Socio-Economic Impact Assessment of Bt Cotton in India

ABOUT THE AUTHORS

T. Haque is a well known Agricultural Economist. He obtained his Ph.D. degree from Patna University (India) and Post Doctoral training from Iowa State University, Ames, U.S.A. Dr. Haque is currently Director, Council for Social Development, New Delhi and Senior Adviser, LANDESA (Rural Development Institute), New Delhi. Earlier he served as Chairman, Commission for Agricultural Costs and Prices, Government of India, ICAR National Fellow at the National Centre for Agricultural Economics and Policy, New Delhi and Director, Centre for Agrarian Studies, NIRD, Hyderabad. He also served as consultant to several international organizations, including FAO, ILO and The World Bank. Dr. Haque is author of six books and about 100 research papers and reports. His areas of specialization are land reform, food security and sustainable agriculture and rural development.

Mondira Bhattacharya is an Associate Fellow at the National Council of Applied Economic Research, New Delhi. She completed her PhD in Agricultural Economics from the Centre for the Study of Regional Development (CSRD), Jawaharlal Nehru University (JNU), New Delhi. Her research interests cover issues in agricultural geography and the impact of related economic policies on the concerned farmer segment. She has several research publications to her credit. Before joining NCAER she had worked at the Confederation of Indian Industry, Council for Social Development and the Institute of Economic Growth, New Delhi, in various capacities.

Ankita Goyal is working as an Associate Fellow at the Council for Social Development, New Delhi. She is completing her PhD from the Centre for Economic Studies and Planning, Jawaharlal Nehru University, New Delhi. She has authored a number of research papers in the field of Agriculture Economics. Her area of specialization is agriculture, food security and sustainable farming.

Socio-Economic Impact Assessment of Bt Cotton in India

T. Haque
Mondira Bhattacharya
Ankita Goyal

Published for
Council for Social Development, New Delhi
by
CONCEPT PUBLISHING COMPANY PVT. LTD.
NEW DELHI-110059

ISBN-13: 978-93-5125-113-2

First Published 2015

Published and Printed by

Concept Since 1974

Concept Publishing Company Pvt. Ltd.
A/15-16, Commercial Block, Mohan Garden
New Delhi-110059 (India)
T: 25351460, 25351794, *F*: 091-11-25357109
E: publishing@conceptpub.com, W: www.conceptpub.com
Editorial Office: H-13, Bali Nagar, New Delhi-110 015, India.

Cataloging in Publication Data--*Courtesy:* D.K. Agencies (P) Ltd. <docinfo@dkagencies.com>

Haque, T. (Tajamul), 1947-
Socio-economic impact assessment of Bt cotton in India / T. Haque, Mondira Bhattacharya, Ankita Goyal.
p. cm.
Includes bibliographical references (p.) and index.
ISBN 9789351251132

1. Cotton growing--India. 2. Cotton growing--Economic aspects--India. 3. Cotton growing--Economic aspects--India--Statistics. 4. Cotton growing--Social aspects--India. 5. Cotton--Genetic engineering--India. 6. Farmers--India--Attitudes. I. Bhattacharya, Mondira, joint author. II. Goyal, Ankita, joint author. III. Title.

DDC 338.17351 23

Acknowledgements

The authors express their sincere thanks to Mr. Ajay Jakhar, President, Bharat Krishak Samaj for sponsoring a study on Socio-Economic Impact Assessment of Bt Cotton in India to the Council for Social Development. In this connection, the support received from Prof. Muchkund Dubey, President of the Council for Social Development in understanding and completing the study in a timely manner is highly appreciated. This is particularly because any discussion on GM crops in India is highly controversial. The authors also benefited immensely from discussion with Dr. Pushpa M. Bhargava, Prof. Abhijit Sen, Dr. G.V. Ramanjaneyulu, Ms. Kavitha Kuruganti, Dr. Anupam Barik, Dr. Chandrasekhar Rao and Dr. Srijit Mishra. Besides, the authors gratefully acknowledge the help received from Mr. Gitesh Sinha, Dr. Swaroop Datta and Ms. Purtika Kalra.

Contents

1

Introduction

The issue whether genetically manipulated crops is good for India and can be adopted in a profitable as well as sustainable manner, keeping in view their productivity potentials and health and environment concerns is not yet resolved. However, the Bt cotton which was introduced in the country in 2002 has gained ground. Now majority of cotton growers in India cultivate this genetically manipulated crop. This book analyses the socio-economic impact of Bt cotton in India.

Cotton is a leading commercial crop grown for its valuable fibre. It is the livelihood of a large number of Indians including 6 million farmers, mostly small and marginal. Cotton provides about 60 per cent of the fibre used in the Indian textile industry, supplies more than a million tonnes of cooking oil, a million tonnes of quality animal feed and about 40 million tonnes of biomass in the form of Cotton stalks (**FICCI 2012**). The crop also accounts for 4 per cent of GDP of the country. Cotton is predominantly grown in nine States which are grouped into three different geographical zones namely, Northern Zone (Punjab, Haryana and Rajasthan), Central Zone (Maharashtra, Madhya Pradesh and Gujarat), and Southern Zone (Andhra Pradesh, Karnataka and Tamil Nadu). It is important to note that majority of the farmers in India are small and marginal (less than 2 hectares of land). According to the Ministry of Agriculture near about 6.3 million farmers planted cotton on 9.04 million hectares in 2008 at an average holding of 1.5 hectares (**Ministry of Agriculture, Government of India, 2007**).

In the year 2011, India ranked number one in the world accounting for 34.05 per cent of the total area planted under Cotton followed by China (15.35%), USA (10.67%) and Pakistan (8.93%). However, even with highest area under Cotton, 12 million hectares, in 2011-12, India ranked second after China in the production of Cotton with 21.54 per cent share, while the production share of China was 27.22 per cent. India's average yield is only 481 kg lint/hec compared to world average of 747.69 kg lint/hec. India's Cotton yield is significantly lower than those of Brazil (1415 kg lint/hec), China (1326 kg lint/hec), USA (886 kg lint/hec) and Pakistan (721 kg lint/hec).

In the aftermath of problems associated with Green Revolution technology in India, agricultural scientists started working on recombinant DNA technology that largely comes under the field of modern biotechnology and genetic engineering. Terms like 'transgenesis' or 'genetic modification' are frequently used to denote this. The crops that are produced by this technology are known as transgenic crops or genetically modified (GM) crops. Scientists claimed it to be the best possible technique to deal with the current agrarian problems like the stagnation in yield, climatic uncertainties and crop diseases, etc. The Cotton crop is highly susceptible to insects and pests, which impact Cotton production. The chemical controls to suppress these insect pests, mainly American Bollworm (*Holicoverpa armegera*), were proving ineffective as they had developed a high level of resistance. The high levels of resistance required repeated application of insecticides leading to heavy expenditure, crop failures, and vicious cycle of debt for farmers. Bt cotton, a transgenic plant, produces an insect controlling toxin Cry1A(c), the gene for which has been derived from the naturally occurring bacterium named *Bacillus Thuringiensis*. It has been argued that adoption of Bt cotton could help in protecting the crop against the most damaging bollworms and thereby reduce the risk of crop failures by reducing chemical insecticide use and providing a major benefit to Cotton growers and the environment.

The first generation GM crop was developed by Monsanto (a multinational company in USA) in 1980s, field tested in early 1990s and released by the government regulators for commercial use in USA in 1996. According to reports of the International Service for the Acquisition of Agri-biotech Applications **(ISAAA) (2010)**, there had been a sharp growth from 1.7 million hectares of GM crops in 1996 to 148 million hectares in 2010 globally – an unprecedented 87 fold increase. In 2010, total 29 countries across the globe cultivated GM crops in which top ten countries who grew more than one million hectares were USA (66.8 million hectares), Brazil (25.4), Argentina (22.9), India (9.4), Canada (8.8), China (3.5), Paraguay (2.6), Pakistan (2.4), South Africa (2.2) and Uruguay (1.1) **(ISAAA 2010).**

India approved its first biotech crop Bt cotton in 2002. It was manufactured and marketed by Monsanto along with its Indian counterpart Mahyco. Only three Bt cotton hybrids (MECH 162 Bt, MECH 184 Bt, and MECH 12 Bt) were approved across six States (Andhra Pradesh, Tamil Nadu, Maharashtra, Gujarat, Madhya Pradesh and Karnataka. In northern zone (Punjab, Haryana and Rajasthan), Bt cotton was approved in 2005. After its commercialization, there was a drastic increase in the rate of adoption and the number of farmers using Bt cotton hybrids across Cotton growing States of India (Chaudhary & Gaur 2010). There was a sharp increase from 50,000 hectares in 2002 to 8.4 million hectares in 2009, representing 168 fold increase in eight years.

It was estimated that only 54,000 farmers grew officially approved Bt cotton hybrids for the first time in 2002. It increased up to 6.4 million farmers over 8.4 million hectares in 2009 (ISAAA Report 2009). In last eight years, various private and government agricultural research institutions and biotech companies developed and diversified the deployment of Bt genes and genotypes. These new Bt genes and genotypes were claimed to be well-adapted to various agro-climatic zones in India ensuring equitable distribution of benefits especially to small and marginal farmers. For instance in 2004, the Central government approved only four Bt cotton hybrids that increased up to 274 in 2008 followed by 522 Bt cotton hybrids in 2009.

Currently the GEAC had granted approval for commercial cultivation of more than 200 Bt cotton hybrids developed by more than 35 seed companies evaluated by public sector organisations. Besides this, there are more than 1,400 event based hybrids featuring three genes and five events developed by four companies, namely, Mahyco Monsanto Biotech (MMB), J.K. Agri Genetics, Nath Seeds and Metahelix.

Currently the Genetic Engineering Approval Committee had granted approval for commercial cultivation of more than 200 Bt cotton hybrids developed by more than 35 seed companies evaluated by public sector organisations. Besides this, there are more than 1,400 event based hybrids featuring three genes and five events developed by four companies, namely, Mahyco Monsanto Biotech (MMB), J.K. Agri Genetics, Nath Seeds and Metahelix. (Ramasundaram *et al.* 2011). Recently the Central Institute of Cotton Research (CICR), a public sector institute, in collaboration with the University of Agricultural Sciences (UAS), Dharwad, had developed a Bt cotton variety—which was the only public sector variety of Bt cotton in India. According to **Herring and Rao (2012)**, this new public sector Bt cotton is an open-pollinated variety, designed to facilitate seed-saving for farmers who prefer to do so. A considerable number of non-approved Bt hybrids are marketed and cultivated in stealth, though a vast proportion of the crop area is under less than half a dozen Bt hybrids.

With a steep increase in the adoption of Bt cotton, the average yield increased from 191 kg/hec in 2002-03 to 517 kg/hectare in 2010-11 across the country. Finally eight consecutive years of good production, India has become transformed from a net importer to a net exporter of Cotton. Export of Cotton has registered a sharp increase from a meagre 0.05 million bales in 2001-02 to 8.8 million bales in 2008-09 (**Choudhary & Gaur 2010**).

Meanwhile, the critics of transgenic technology correlated Bt cotton cultivation with, the ongoing farmer suicides across Cotton growing States of India, rising cost of cultivation and monopoly of private sector seed companies like Mahyco-Monsanto.

Shah and Banerji (2002) highlighted the fact that the sole idea behind introducing Bt cotton was that it would raise the net income of farmers by reducing spending on pesticides. However, they said that spending on pesticides had not reduced as 20 per cent of Bt fields needed to be covered with Non-Bt seeds (to ensure that pest resistance to Bt cotton does not rapidly develop), that required use of pesticides. Moreover, seed costs for Bt cotton were much higher than Non-Bt.

Bhargava (2003), questioned as to why Indian biotechnology organizations like Department of Biotechnology did not develop commercial genetic engineering in India and that allowing Monsanto's Bt cotton technology seemed to be deliberate. He also identified several risks involved in the release of genetically modified (GM) crops and the damage such a release could cause to human and animal health and the environment. He argued that all necessary tests (risk assessment tests) had not been carried out in the public domain before arriving at the decision to approve Bt cotton for commercial cultivation in India. Further he feels that India had 'deliberately' not used alternatives to Bt cotton for minimising pest attacks. For example, Integrated Pest Management (IPM) had been successfully developed and tested for Cotton by the Ministry of Agriculture years ago. However, this had not been used in the country as extensively as it should have been. Similarly, the government did not encourage the use of natural Cotton varieties which would be less susceptible to pests or of traditional or modern agricultural practices that would bring down the use of pesticides. Moreover, he claimed that no farmer was told during the trials that resistance to Bt would gradually develop in the pests and that the farmers would need to put in some 50 per cent refuge crop at the end of five years or so of use of Monsanto-Mahyco's Bt cotton seeds. On the issue of field trials of Bt cotton, **Bhargava (2009)** claims that so far such field trials have not been conducted properly. They have been conducted without appropriate professional approval of the State Government and that they had been done either by the GMO applicants themselves or by organisations to which samples were supplied by the applicants.

Explaining farmer suicides in the State of Maharashtra, **Mitra & Shroff (2007)** said that overall, three factors contributed to the plight of farmers, namely low Cotton yields exposed to the lower international prices after liberalisation, a lack of dynamism in Cotton yield per hectare in a dynamic world and a huge increase in costs of cultivation. All these factors made Cotton farming unremunerative. In the case of Maharashtra, there was a suicide epidemic in recent times because the mentioned imbalances were large enough to lead to a decline in profit incomes to levels, which were significantly negative. One recent factor leading to an increase in the cost of cultivation is the use of costly Bt cotton seeds by farmers.

Kavitha Kuruganti (2009), questioned the discourse about GM crops in India that was willing to accept blindly that Bt cotton was the reason for yield increases in Cotton in India. She argued that large-scale shift in seed sources, shift from unirrigated to irrigated Cotton, good monsoons, low pest incidence, and increased use of chemical fertilisers had actually contributed to Cotton yield increases in some years in some States of the country.

Glenn Davis Stone (2012) points out to some 'ugly facts' revolving around the so called remarkable success of Bt cotton in India as hailed by ISAAA. He claimed that firstly, most of the yield increases in Bt cotton happened between the years 2002 and 2005 when Bt cotton comprised between 0.4 to 5.6 per cent of India's Cotton. Secondly, in the last four years as Bt rose from 67 per cent to 92 per cent of India's Cotton, yields had dropped steadily. Thirdly, in Gujarat, the State that recorded highest yields, there were many factors contributing to cotton yields other than Bt, namely bringing new areas under Cotton cultivation, involving fertile soils that were previously under groundnut cultivation, micro-irrigation systems, and use of new pesticides.

Gaurav and Mishra (2012) conducted a random sample of Bt cotton growers from Gujarat and Maharashtra in drought year 2009-10 and compared it with the data in 2002, another drought year. In this article, they argued about risk considerations of Bt cotton. They said that yield variability of Bt cotton was higher. Assuming this as an indicator of inter-temporal variability in yield, farmers who had not yet chosen Bt cotton, may be inferred to have had a preference for reliability of the yields which the non-Bt cotton varieties could be offering. If farmers chose stability and lower fluctuations in yield to higher expected returns (yield), their risk avoidance behaviour in terms of not choosing Bt cotton seeds was indeed rational.

Despite criticism, there have been several proponents of the Bt technology in India. **Naik** *et al.* **(2005)**, carried out a survey in four Cotton growing States of India, namely Maharashtra, Karnataka, Andhra Pradesh, and Tamil Nadu with a sample of 341 farmers. They concluded that on an average, Bt technology leads to significant pesticide reductions, yield gains, and income increases. There was a reduction in pesticide spraying by 2.6 times against the major insect pests, than the conventional varieties. The toxin encoded by Bt gene Cry1A(c) does not provide any protection against sucking pest, virus, bacteria and fungi. Even the protection against certain bollworm species (like spotted bollworm, tobacco bollworm, pink bollworm, etc.) was less than 100 per cent. But most of the available published data showed that Bt cotton successfully reduced the attack of American bollworm. They further commented that advantage of Bt technology was its positive impact on yield as a result of lower crop losses. However, not every single adopter benefited, because there is a high degree of heterogeneity among farmers in terms of agroecological and socio-economic conditions. Whether or not Bt technology is appropriate for a particular farmer depends on (i) local pest pressure, (ii) individual crop management, and (iii) local suitability of the germplasm into which the Bt gene is incorporated. They reiterated that seed suppliers should properly inform farmers on how to use the technology successfully. Further they confirmed that the increasing demand for Bt seeds in India and the rapidly increasing rates of diffusion clearly demonstrate that the technology is beneficial for the majority of Cotton farmers.

Blaise and **Kranthi (2011)**, studied toxicity levels of Bt cotton in soils in India and found that soil moisture stress (excess or deficit) had an adverse effect on toxin production. Such soil moisture stress in the cultivation of transgenic crops such as Bt cotton has serious implications such as ineffective pest control, pest becoming resistant to Bt toxin and high pesticide use.

According to **Pray** *et al.* **(2005)**, Bt cotton showed increased returns by way of savings in plant protection and a higher yield through averting yield loss. However, there were higher seed costs and picking expenditure.

Interestingly, there has been an increasing trend in the adoption of multiple gene Bt cotton hybrids.[1] It has been mentioned earlier that in a study conducted by **Naik** *et al.* **in 2005**, it was found that the toxin encoded by Bt gene Cry1A(c) did not provide any protection against sucking pest, virus, bacteria and fungi and even certain bollworm species. Of late, Bt cotton was also largely attacked by a new pest called 'mealy bug' in various parts of India, as well as an increasing incidence of attacks of aphids, jassids, thrips and white fly **(Goswami 2007)**. In response to this multiple gene Bt cotton hybrids were introduced. These were first developed by Mahyco-Monsanto Biotech (MMB) and the hybrid was popularly known as Bollgard II or BG II.

According to **G.V. Ramanjaneyulu** after some time the bollworm would again become resistant to BG-II and the company would then introduce BG-III (*The Hindu* 2010). According to the report of Hindu Business Line (2010), Monsanto had already begun to work on two new technologies – Bollgard III (the third generation Bt technology) and Roundup Ready Flex (a technology that gives herbicide tolerance to plant).

Meanwhile, India's first indigenous publicly bred Bt cotton variety *Bikaneri Narma* (BN) and hybrid NHH-44Bt (expressing event BNLA-601) were developed and commercialized in 2009 by a group of public sector institutions, namely, Central Institute for Cotton Research (CICR Nagpur), National Research Centre for Plant Biotechnology **(NRCPB, New Delhi)**, Indian Council of Agricultural Research (ICAR New Delhi) in partnership with University of Agricultural Sciences (UAS Dhadwad, Karnataka). However, according to the Coalition for GM free India (2011), these public sector Bt cotton lines is actually found to have a Bt gene originally patented by Monsanto.

Ramasundaram *et al.* **(2011)**, primarily focused on the issue of whether it is necessary to grow hybrids in order to benefit from Bt cotton. They stated that Bt cotton hybrids had resulted in elimination of true varieties. Promoting Bt cotton hybrids was an illusion being created by the private sector to extract surplus through the sale of seed. This is in sharp contrast to the spread of Bt cotton elsewhere in the world where no hybrids were used. Moreover despite the dominance of hybrids, the current productivity of Cotton in India was far below that of USA and China, which cultivated only true varieties and not hybrids. They said that there is a need to revive the cultivation of true varieties and this poses a challenge to the public sector.

The study by **Mayer and Choudhary** (2013), in the states of Maharashtra, Andhra Pradesh and Punjab revealed that the overall economics of Bt Cotton cultivation was favourable to cotton farmers.

Objectives of this Study

The specific objectives of this study were as follows:

1. To undertake a spatial and temporal analysis of World Cotton production and trade.
2. To analyse trends in area, production, yields and farm input use in cotton in India.
3. To undertake cost of cultivation and net return analysis of Bt cotton in different States across farm size categories.
4. To analyse the agronomic factors which influence Bt cotton yields.
5. To analyse the effect of incomes of Bt cotton on the health and sanitation, education and other livelihood status of farmers.
6. To analyse the impact of Bt cotton on labour employment and income of landless labourers.
7. To find out the perception of the farmers about various positive and negative aspects of Bt cotton cultivation.

Database

The study was based on secondary as well as primary data for the major Cotton growing States in India namely, Andhra Pradesh, Haryana, Punjab, Madhya Pradesh, Maharashtra, Gujarat, Rajasthan, Tamil Nadu and Karnataka.

Most of the secondary data and information for the latest years available at the national, State and district levels, on area, yields, prices and cost of cultivation were collected from the Directorate of Economics and Statistics, Ministry of Agriculture and Cooperation, Government of India. International data on crop and trade statistics was collected from United States Department of Agriculture (USDA), United Nations Conference on Trade and Development (UNCTAD) and FAOSTAT. For the purpose of preliminary farm level data, a household survey was conducted in all nine major cotton growing States for the agricultural year 2010-11. Districts from each State were purposively selected on the basis of secondary data on area under cotton. More than one district was taken from States which showed high acreage under cotton crop (average cotton area between 2000-01 and 2006-07). Accordingly, 2 districts each from Maharashtra, Gujarat, Andhra Pradesh, Madhya Pradesh, Punjab and Haryana and one district each from Karnataka, Rajasthan and Tamil Nadu were chosen (Table 1.1).

Table 1.1: Districts Selected for Primary Survey

States	*Districts with High Proportion of Area under Cotton (Average of 2000-01 to 2006-07)*	
	Districts	*Area (%)*
Punjab	Bathinda	27.74
	Ferozpur	25.32
Haryana	Sirsa	32.15
	Hisar	26.19
Rajasthan	Hanumangarh	43.36
Gujarat	Surendranagar	24.14
	Bhavnagar	11.58
Maharashtra	Jalgaon	13.05
	Yavatmal	12.94
Madhya Pradesh	Khargone	30.90
	Dhar	17.00
Andhra Pradesh	Adilabad	16.80
	Warangal	14.73
Karnataka	Dharwad	18.21
Tamil Nadu	Virudunagar	14.31

Source: Directorate of Economics and Statistics, Ministry of Agriculture & Cooperation, GoI.

Further, a Block and a cluster of 5 villages from each block were chosen in consultation with local Block level officers. 70 farm households from each of the selected Block/cluster of 5 villages were selected forming a total sample of 1,050 farm households for the study. Apart from this 20 local agricultural labourers from each district, considering 10 males and 10 females from each district were also interviewed. Further, farming households in each Block were divided into 3 categories based on their owned operational holdings into small (less than 2 hectares), medium (between 2 and 4 hectares) and large (above 4 hectares). A detailed questionnaire schedule was then prepared for the collection of primary data.

Methodology

The present study is a cross-sectional analysis of farming population for a single year and hence the information received has been compared with secondary data received from Government sources. Since it is difficult to compare a single year study with previous years using the same population dataset, hence, farmers' recall method has been used during the interview. Further, a lot of information is based on farmers' perception regarding various issues.

Apart from this various mathematical and statistical techniques were used to analyse data and to interpret results. These tools included tabular and graphical analysis, trend growth rates using semi-log function, coefficient of variation, correlations and regressions.

Cost of Cultivation

To understand the economics of cotton production, an analysis of cost of cultivation was undertaken. Data collected through field survey was used extensively for the detailed analysis. The present study follows the methodology adopted by the Directorate of Economics and Statistics, Ministry of Agriculture, Government of India in its annual report 'Comprehensive Scheme for Studying the Cost of Cultivation of Principal Crops in India'.

Productivity Function

The ordinary least squares (OLS) estimates of Bt cotton productivity was carried out through a productivity function. In this function the variables were taken in relative terms wherein each variable was divided by the Bt cotton crop area. The variables were then expressed in logarithmic form to introduce linearity. The log linear transformation of this productivity function is stated as follows:

$$\log Bt\,CGVO = \log C + b_1 \log NCA + b_2 \log HL + b_3 \log MH + b_4 \log S + b_5 \log F + b_6 \log P + b_7 \log GR + b_8 \log FYM + b_9 \log M + b_{10} \log I$$

where,

Bt CGVO_hc = Gross value of output of Bt cotton (₹/hec)
NCA = Net cultivated area (hec)
HL_hec = Human labour use (₹/Hec)
MH_hec = Mechanisation cost (₹/Hec)
S_hec = Seed costs (₹/Hec)
F_hec = Fertilizer costs (₹/Hec)
P_hec = Pesticide costs (₹/Hec)
GR_hec = Growth regulator costs (₹/Hec)
FYM_hec = Farmyard manure costs (₹/Hec)
M_hec = Micronutrient costs (₹/Hec)
I_hec = Irrigation costs (₹/Hec)

Growth Rates using Semi-Log Function

The equation of Semi-log Function is $Y_t = \alpha\beta^t$

where,

'y' is the dependent variable for which growth rate is estimated
't' is time variable
'β' is regression coefficient
'α' is intercept.

The growth rate 'r' is obtained from the logarithmic form of the equation as follows:

$$\log y = \log a + t \log b.$$

Thereafter the growth rate ('r' in%) is calculated as:

$$r = [(\text{Antilog of log b}) - 1]*100$$

Scheme of Chapterisation

Chapter 1: Introduction
Chapter 2: Spatio-Temporal Analysis of World Cotton Production and Trade
Chapter 3: Trends in Area, Production, Yield, Prices and Input Use
Chapter 4: Economics of Cost of Cultivation of Bt Cotton—Results of Farm Level Survey

Chapter 5:	Factors Influencing Bt Cotton Yields
Chapter 6:	Farmers' Perception on the Impact of Bt Cotton on Income, Health and Livelihood Status
Chapter 7:	Impact of Bt Cotton on Labour Employment and Income of Landless Labourers
Chapter 8:	Key Findings and Conclusions

Note

1. The event MON15985 contains two genes (Cry 1Ac and Cry 1Ab) that is responsible to provide additional protection to Spodoptera (leaf-eating tobacco caterpillar) while it also increased the efficacy of the protection to American Bollworm, Pink Bollworm and Spotted Bollworm.

2

Spatio-Temporal Analysis of World Cotton Production and Trade

Cotton is an important fibre crop of global significance, which is universally used as a textile raw material. It is cultivated in tropical and sub-tropical regions of more than 100 countries the world over. It is a heavily traded agricultural commodity, with over 150 countries involved in exports or imports of Cotton. Currently the largest producing countries are China, India, USA, Pakistan, Brazil and Australia. These countries contributed about 81 per cent to the global Cotton production in 2012. India has the largest acreage (around 11.8 million hectares) under Cotton at global level and has the productivity of 489 kg lint/Hec and ranks second in share of production (21.98%) after China during (28.91%) in 2012.

This chapter provides a spatial and temporal analysis of international cotton production and trade and the position of India *vis-à-vis* the world.

Area under Cotton in the World

Over the last 5 decades, India has occupied the largest share of Cotton area in the world (above 20%), and in 2012 it increased to 34.52 per cent (Table 2.1). India is followed by China and USA. The share of China in Cotton area was 15.71 per cent in 1970-71 which increased to 16.86 per cent in 1990 but reduced to 15.50 per cent in 2012. The area share of USA was 14.19 per cent in 1970-71 which was reduced to 11.09 per cent in 2012. The other major shareholders in the recent decade are Pakistan, Uzbekistan, Brazil, Turkmenistan, Burkina, Mali and Tanzania. (Table 2.1).

Trends in Average Cotton Yields in Different Countries

It would be seen from Table 2.2 that, over the last 5 decades, some of the countries that showed high yields of cotton consistently were Israel, Australia

Table 2.1: Percentage Share of Various Countries in the Area under Cotton in the World

Countries	1970	Countries	1980	Countries	1990	Countries	2000	Countries	2012
India	23.92	India	24.17	India	22.44	India	26.80	India	34.52
China	15.71	USA	16.52	China	16.86	USA	16.51	China	15.50
USA	14.19	China	15.20	USA	14.32	China	12.68	United States	11.09
USSR	8.64	USSR	9.72	Pakistan	8.03	Pakistan	9.15	Pakistan	8.78
Brazil	7.76	Pakistan	6.52	Brazil	5.96	Uzbekistan	4.45	Uzbekistan	3.85
Pakistan	5.50	Brazil	6.23	Uzbekistan	5.52	Brazil	2.67	Brazil	2.59
Uganda	2.54	Turkey	2.08	Turkey	1.93	Turkey	2.04	Turkmenistan	1.76
Egypt	2.15	Egypt	1.62	Argentina	1.90	Australia	1.58	Burkina	1.70
Turkey	1.65	Sudan	1.20	Turkmenistan	1.88	Turkmenistan	1.48	Mali	1.53
Sudan	1.60	Tanzania	1.20	Paraguay	1.69	Greece	1.28	Tanzania	1.46

Source: USDA

and Mexico (above 1300 kg lint/hec). In recent years, countries such as Turkey, Brazil, Mexico, China, Syria, Venezuela, Bulgaria and Tunisia have also reported high yields. The Cotton yields of India have been comparatively less. In 2012 it was 491 kg lint/hec which was less than the world average of 763 kg/lint per hectare and also much lesser than the top yielding countries.

Table 2.2: Average Cotton Yields in Different Countries (kg/hec)

Countries	1970	Countries	1980	Countries	1990	Countries	2000	Countries	2012
Israel	995	Israel	1261	Israel	1658	Israel	1633	Australia	2351
El Salvador	864	Guatemala	1217	Australia	1552	Australia	1595	Israel	1773
USSR	854	Australia	1179	Bulgaria	1256	Syria	1351	Mexico	1512
Greece	833	Egypt	1011	Guatemala	1070	Turkey	1198	China	1438
Nicaragua	830	Mexico	965	Turkey	1021	Venezuela	1161	Brazil	1427
Australia	784	Spain	930	Albania	998	Brazil	1101	Turkey	1381
Guatemala	781	USSR	858	Honduras	980	China	1089	Syria	1263
Turkey	760	Syria	849	Spain	936	Tunisia	1089	Venezuela	1234
Mexico	748	Greece	820	Syria	930	Greece	1081	Bulgaria	1089
Egypt	744	Nicaragua	806	Costa Rica	871	Mexico	1059	Tunisia	1089

Source: USDA

World Cotton Trade

In this chapter India's position in world Cotton trade has been studied over two time periods based on starting year of commercial cultivation of Bt cotton in India i.e., 2002-03. It may be seen from Table 2.3, that in both the Pre-Bt cotton (1995-96 to 2001-02) and Post-Bt cotton period (2002-03 to 2012), USA was the largest exporter of Cotton in quantity terms ('000 tonnes) followed by Uzbekistan (Table 2.3). India joined the major exporters list only in the Post-Bt cotton period, surpassing Uzbekistan (8.67%) and contributing about 11.90 per cent to the world export, USA securing 36.49 per cent of the share. The other main stakeholders between 2002-03 and 2012-13 were Australia, Brazil, Greece, Burkina Faso, Mali, Turkmenistan and Tajikistan.

Table 2.3: Share in World Cotton Exports by Major Exporting Countries (%)

Countries	*Pre-Bt cotton Period (1995-96 to 2001-02)*	*Countries*	*Post-Bt cotton Period (2002-03 to 2012-13)*
United States of America	27.38	United States of America	36.49
Uzbekistan	14.85	India	11.90
Australia	10.55	Uzbekistan	8.67
Greece	4.34	Australia	7.37
Argentina	3.98	Brazil	5.91
Turkmenistan	3.00	Greece	3.08
Syrian Arab Republic	2.84	Burkina Faso	2.25
Mali	2.62	Mali	2.10
Benin	2.10	Turkmenistan	1.68
Côte d'Ivoire	1.98	Tajikistan	1.45

Source: FAOSTAT and UNCTAD.

The major importing countries (Table 2.4) in both the Pre and Post Bt cotton period were China, Turkey, Thailand, Mexico, Republic of Korea, Russian Federation and Italy. Among these China was the major importing country followed by Turkey and Indonesia. In case of India, it was seen that, Cotton exports have been more than its imports. India shared about 2.19 per cent of world imports and contributed 8.60 per cent to world exports.

Table 2.4: Share in World Cotton Exports by Major Importing Countries (%)

Countries	*Pre-Bt cotton Period (1995-96 to 2001-02)*	*Countries*	*Post-Bt cotton Period (2002-03 to 2012-13)*
China	10.77	China	34.65
Indonesia	8.84	Turkey	8.93
Turkey	5.79	Indonesia	7.00
Brazil	5.62	Bangladesh	5.80
Thailand	5.55	Pakistan	4.92
Republic of Korea	5.46	Mexico	4.42
Italy	5.46	Thailand	3.88
Mexico	5.08	Republic of Korea	3.33
Japan	4.98	Vietnam	3.13
Russian Federation	3.77	Russian Federation	2.50

Source: FAOSTAT and UNCTAD

Cotton Trade of India

India is a major cotton exporter and in the recent years it has been annually exporting about 1 million tonnes, accounting for nearly 10 per cent of agricultural exports and close to 5 per cent in quantity terms (Table 2.5). As regards imports it is noticed that, in recent years India has been annually importing about 0.1 million tonnes, accounting for around 1 per cent of the total quantum of agricultural imports quantity terms and over 2 per cent of that in value terms.

Table 2.5: Exports and Imports of Cotton lint as a Proportion of Total Agricultural Exports and Imports (%)

Cotton Trade of India	*TE-1991*	*TE-1994*	*TE-1997*	*TE-2000*	*TE-2003*	*TE-2006*	*TE-2009*
Exports Quantities (%)	3.21	1.34	1.13	0.20	0.37	3.28	4.50
Exports Value (%)	7.42	3.29	3.88	0.43	1.04	7.48	9.47
Imports Quantities (%)	0.09	1.60	0.68	2.15	3.19	0.91	1.06
Imports Value (%)	0.30	5.46	2.74	6.01	8.10	3.06	2.84

Source: Economic Survey.

Table 2.6: Share of Value of Agricultural Commodities Exports in Total Agro-Exports of India (%)

Agriculture & Allied Activities	*TE-1982*	*TE-1985*	*TE-1988*	*TE-1991*	*TE-1994*	*TE-1997*	*TE-2000*	*TE-2003*	*TE-2006*	*TE-2009*
Raw Cotton	**5.14**	**3.86**	**3.56**	**7.44**	**2.98**	**2.98**	**0.75**	**1.30**	**7.77**	**10.53**
Rice	12.70	6.52	8.82	9.18	10.29	10.29	18.34	16.35	16.58	16.82
Coffee	8.94	8.53	8.74	5.41	6.02	6.02	6.42	3.94	3.82	3.01
Tea & Mate	19.42	24.79	18.30	18.33	9.22	9.22	8.87	6.21	4.58	3.73
Oil Cakes	6.32	5.57	8.16	12.10	17.32	17.32	8.26	9.28	11.19	12.86
Tobacco	9.94	6.90	4.60	4.56	3.65	3.65	3.88	3.63	3.52	4.68
Cashew Kernels	7.41	7.21	9.46	8.34	9.30	9.30	8.77	6.69	6.27	3.89
Spices	3.16	7.71	9.16	5.18	4.81	4.81	7.35	5.82	5.90	8.16
Sugar & Molasses	2.72	3.16	0.23	1.17	1.83	1.83	0.81	5.97	3.29	5.27
Fish & Fish Preparations	13.81	15.08	17.38	17.17	23.91	23.91	23.19	23.44	17.76	11.64
Meat & Meat Preparations	3.46	3.00	2.63	2.69	2.77	2.77	4.48	5.32	6.58	7.46
Fruits	5.39	4.78	4.63	4.31	4.46	4.46	5.52	6.97	8.85	7.79
Miscellaneous	1.59	2.89	4.33	4.11	3.44	3.44	3.36	5.11	3.88	4.15

Source: Calculated from data on Exports of Agriculture and Allied Activities, *Economic Survey*, Various Issues.
Note: TE–Triennium Ending.

Some of the key trends that are noticed from both the above Tables 2.5 and 2.6 are that, the contribution of Cotton in India's agro-export both in quantity and value terms had plummeted during the nineties and grew significantly during the first decade of the new millennium. Its share in the value of export from the country in recent years (10.53%) has been preceded by rice (16.82%), oilcakes (12.86%) and fish and fish preparations (11.64%).

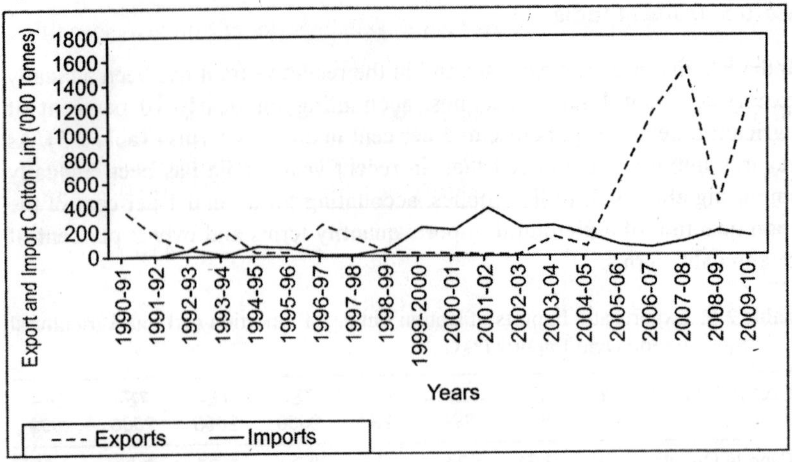

Source: Economic Survey.

Fig. 2.1: Exports and Imports of Cotton lint ('000 Tonnes)

From Figure 2.1, it is seen that Cotton exports started to increase from 2002-03 onwards. It reached 599 thousand tonnes in 2005-06 and continued to climb in subsequent seasons (1144, 1531 thousand tonnes in 2006-07 and 2007-08, respectively). In 2008-09 it declined to 440 thousand tonnes, but increased to 1,328 thousand tonnes in 2009-10. India's Cotton exports dropped in 2008-09 due to several reasons such as,

- less production caused by uneven rainfall coupled with high pest incidence that could have affected Cotton productivity,
- low international prices in the aftermath of the world financial crises, and
- decreased value of rupee against the dollar that affected Cotton exports.

Imports have risen slightly. Imports were high at the turn of the century (385 thousand tonnes in 2001-02) but dropped due to the rapid expansion of the domestic Cotton industry. However as of July 2008, the Government of India abolished the duty on Cotton imports into the country boosting imports to 196 thousand tonnes in 2008-09.

Further, from Table 2.7 it is seen that, the trend growth rate of Cotton exports in quantity terms was –24.6 and in value terms it was –21.3 per cent between 1990-91 and 2001-02. However these export trends increased significantly to above 75 per cent between the period 2002-03 and 2009-10. This can be largely attributed to the advent of Bt cotton in India. The advent of Bt cotton has changed India from being a net importer of Cotton as seen till the year ending 2001-02 to being a net exporter of Cotton.

Table 2.7: Trend Growth Rates in Export and Import of Cotton (%)

India	*Pre-Bt cotton Period (1990-91 to 2001-02)*	*Post-Bt cotton Period (2002-03 to 2009-10)*
Quantity of Exports (tonnes)	–24.6	75.1
Value of Exports (1000 US$)	–21.3	80.9
Quantity of Imports (tonnes)	64.3	–6.3
Value of Imports (1000 US$)	49.5	0.4

Source: Economic Survey.

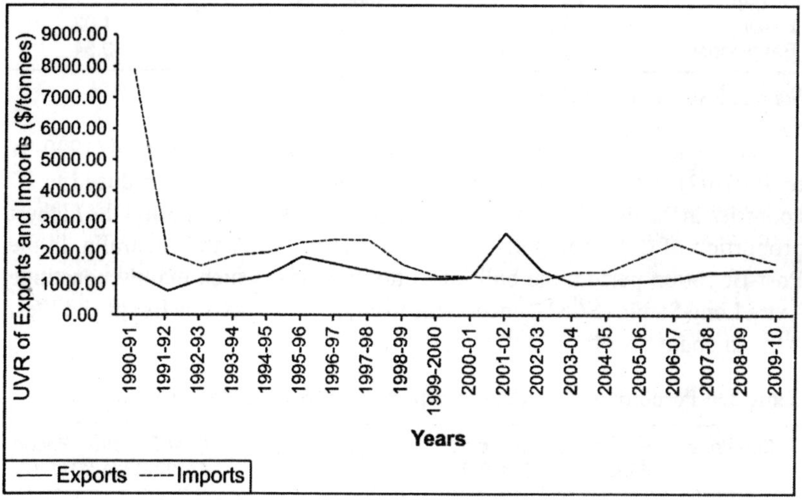

Source: Economic Survey.

Fig. 2.2: Unit Value Realisation of Exports and Imports of Cotton lint (US$/tonne)

Figure 2.2 shows that, over the years unit value realization from imports have been more than exports. Ever since a major slump from 1990 to 1991, import prices of Cotton over the years have shown a trend growth rate of –2.89 per cent. In case of export prices, the trend has been quite stable with a slight increase of 2618.18 US$/tonne in the year 2001-02. The trend growth rate was 0.62 per cent.

In the Pre-Bt cotton period (1990-91 to 2001-02) India exported Cotton to 75 countries and it increased to 84 countries in the Post-Bt cotton period (2002-03 to 2011-12). From Table 2.8 it is seen that in the Pre-Bt cotton period, largest proportion of Cotton exports from India went to Hongkong, Japan and Indonesia. However, in the Post-Bt cotton period the bulk of the country's Cotton exports went to China, followed by Pakistan, Bangladesh and other Far-East countries.

Table 2.8: Proportion of Cotton Lint Exports to Major Countries from India (%)

Countries	Pre-Bt cotton Period (1990-91 to 2001-02)	Countries	Post-Bt cotton Period (2002-03 to 2011-12)
Hong Kong	16.86	China	54.77
Japan	12.80	Pakistan	14.21
Indonesia	10.08	Bangladesh	11.71
Thailand	9.20	Indonesia	4.39
USSR	8.67	Vietnam	3.03
China	8.09	Turkey	2.72
Spain	5.37	Thailand	2.42
Singapore	4.21	Hong Kong	2.21
Brazil	2.70	Malaysia	1.02
Bangladesh	2.32	Mauritius	0.54

Source: FAOSTAT and UNCTAD.

As regards Cotton imports to India, in the Pre-Bt cotton period (1990-91 to 2001-02) India imported Cotton from 99 countries and it reduced to 77 countries in the Post-Bt cotton period. In the Pre-Bt Cotton period the highest proportion of Cotton imports to India were from USA and Australia. In the Post-Bt cotton period, the bulk of Cotton imports, which mainly constitute Extra Long Staple (ELS) Cotton came from USA followed by Egypt and West African countries (Table 2.9).

Table 2.9: Proportion of Cotton lint Imports to India from Major Countries (%)

Countries	Pre-Bt cotton Period (1990-91 to 2001-02)	Countries	Post-Bt cotton Period (2002-03 to 2011-12)
USA	18.34	USA	32.83
Australia	11.12	Egypt	16.32
Egypt	7.09	Tanzania	6.97
Benin	6.26	Mali	4.42
Côte d'Ivoire	5.80	Burkina Faso	3.91
Uzbekistan	3.97	Uzbekistan	3.14
Pakistan	3.83	Benin	2.95
South Africa	2.95	Sudan	2.94
Turkey	2.84	Greece	2.90
Sudan	2.73	Australia	2.46

Source: FAOSTAT and UNCTAD.

The bulk of the India's cotton exports went to China, followed by Pakistan, Bangladesh and other Far-East countries, while the bulk of cotton imports, which mainly constitute Extra Long Staple (ELS) cotton came from USA followed by Egypt and West African countries.

3

Trends in Area, Production, Yield, Prices and Input Use

The planting period of cotton in India takes place from March to September (kharif), while harvesting takes place from October to February (rabi). cotton is produced in three zones, the northern zone comprising the States of Punjab, Haryana and Rajasthan, the central zone comprising the States of Maharashtra, Madhya Pradesh and Gujarat and the southern zone comprising the States of Andhra Pradesh, Karnataka and Tamil Nadu. Besides these 9 States, cotton cultivation is gaining momentum in the State of Orissa. About 70 per cent of total cotton production is accounted by the States of Gujarat, Maharashtra and Andhra Pradesh. India has the largest area devoted to cotton cultivation (12.20 million hectares in 2011-12) with an estimated 6 million farms. Approximately 65 per cent of India's cotton is produced in rain-fed areas. India is the only country to grow all four species of cultivated cotton *Gossypium arboreum* and *Gossypium herbaceum* (Asian Cotton), *Gossypium barbadense* (Egyptian Cotton) and *Gossypium hirsutum* (American Upland Cotton). *Gossypium hirsutum* represents 90 per cent of the hybrid cotton production in India. India produces a large number of cotton varieties and hybrids. Though the number of varieties in cultivation exceeded 75, about 98 per cent of the production was contributed by about 25 varieties. The rapid growth in yields after 2002-03 has been attributed to the introduction and expansion of Bt cotton hybrids, improved crop management practices and overall favourable weather conditions in most of the States involved. According to recent studies, with the area under Bt cotton and improved varieties nearly peaking, the prospect for future growth in productivity is limited as most cotton is grown under rain fed conditions and on landholdings of small size. Moreover, in recent years the yields have shown some stagnation, necessitating an in-depth enquiry into the study of this crop, to understand reasons for such yield stagnations. With this background this chapter focuses on the trends in area, production and yields as well as input usage and prices of cotton in India.

Table 3.1: All India Area, Production and Yield of Cotton

Year	Area (lakh hectares)	Production (lakh bales of 170 kgs each	Yield (kg lint/ hec)	Year	Area (lakh hectares)	Production (lakh bales of 170 kgs each	Yield (kg lint/hec)
1950-51	59	30	88	**1982-83**	79	75	163
1951-52	66	33	85	**1983-84**	77	64	141
1952-53	64	33	89	**1984-85**	74	85	196
1953-54	70	41	100	**1985-86**	75	87	197
1954-55	76	45	100	**1986-87**	70	69	169
1955-56	81	42	88	**1987-88**	65	64	168
1956-57	80	49	104	**1988-89**	73	87	202
1957-58	80	50	105	**1989-90**	77	114	252
1958-59	80	49	104	**1990-91**	74	98	225
1959-60	73	37	86	**1991-92**	77	97	215
1960-61	76	56	125	**1992-93**	75	114	257
1961-62	80	49	103	**1993-94**	73	107	249
1962-63	77	55	122	**1994-95**	79	119	257
1963-64	82	58	119	**1995-96**	90	129	242
1964-65	84	60	122	**1996-97**	91	142	265
1965-66	80	49	104	**1997-98**	89	109	208
1966-67	78	53	114	**1998-99**	93	165	302
1967-68	80	58	123	**1999-00**	87	156	304
1968-69	76	55	122	**2000-01**	86	140	277
1969-70	77	56	122	**2001-02**	87	158	308
1970-71	76	48	106	**2002-03**	77	136	301
1971-72	78	70	151	**2003-04**	76	179	399
1972-73	77	57	127	**2004-05**	88	243	470
1973-74	76	63	142	**2005-06**	87	244	478
1974-75	76	72	161	**2006-07**	91	280	521
1975-76	74	60	138	**2007-08**	95	310	553
1976-77	69	58	144	**2008-09**	94	290	524
1977-78	79	72	156	**2009-10**	103	305	503
1978-79	81	80	167	**2010-11**	111	339	517
1979-80	81	77	160	**2011-12**	122	345	481
1980-81	78	70	152	**CAGR 1950-2011 (%)**	**0.42**	**3.38**	**2.94**
1981-82	81	79	166	**CAGR 1950-2001 (%)**	**0.26**	**2.69**	**2.42**
				CAGR 2002-2011 (%)	**4.91**	**9.25**	**4.15**

Source: Central Institute for Cotton Research, Cotton Advisory Board and Ministry of Agriculture, GoI.

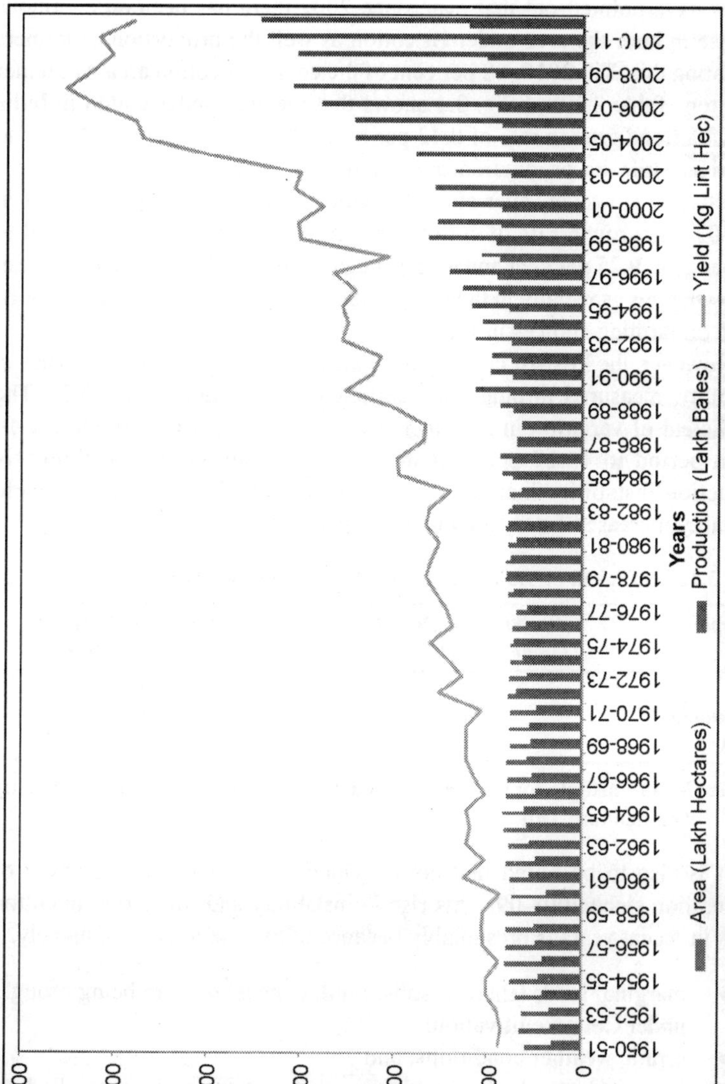

Source: Central Institute for Cotton Research, Cotton Advisory Board and Ministry of Agriculture, GoI

Fig. 3.1: All India Area, Production and Yield of Cotton

Bt cotton in India was introduced in the year 2002 and the Bt period starting from 2002-03 and continuing today, brought about a significant increase in the growth of cotton acreage, production and productivity. Many studies have pointed out that ever since 2002 there has been an enormous increase in both the area under Bt cotton as well the proportion of farmers cultivating this. Till 2010, 88 per cent of the country's cotton area was under Bt cotton. Table 3.1 and Fig. 3.1 shows that the area under cotton in India grew at a trend growth rate of 0.42 per cent between the years 1950-51 and 2011-12, while its production and yield grew at 3.38 and 2.94 per cent respectively. However, ever since the cultivation of Bt cotton in India in 2002-03, the growth rate of cotton area, production and yield increased to 4.91per cent, 9.25 per cent and 4.15 per cent respectively. This quantum leap in growth rates especially in the last decade suggests the huge influence of Bt cotton on farming choices in India.

However, the Post-Bt cotton period also registered a marked increase in instability, measured through the coefficient of variation (Table 3.2). The co-efficient of variation in area increased from 8.71 per cent in the Pre-Bt cotton period to 15.27 per cent in the Post-Bt cotton period. Similarly production instability increased from 18.74 to 25.35 per cent and yield instability increased from 13.09 to 15.57 per cent.

Table 3.2: Coefficient of Variation of Area, Production and Yield (%)

Parameters	*Pre-Bt cotton Period (1990-91 to 2001-02)*	*Post-Bt cotton Period (2002-03 to 2011-12)*
Area	8.71	15.27
Production	18.74	25.35
Yield	13.09	15.57

Source: Central Institute for Cotton Research, Cotton Advisory Board and Ministry of Agriculture, GoI

It is also to be noted that cotton yields show signs of stagnation or deceleration since 2008-09. This rise in instability and stagnation in cotton yields in recent years is presumably because of two main reasons, namely:

- marginal lands (shallow soils, rainfed areas) that are being brought under Cotton cultivation;
- erratic weather conditions; and
- increased attacks by sucking pests not sufficiently controlled by insecticides or current Bt technologies.

It may be seen from Table 3.3 that the proportion of irrigated area under cotton, i.e., cotton irrigated area as a proportion of total cotton area, increased substantially from 8.2 per cent in 1950-51 to 28.89 per cent in 2011-12. However, it remained at around 34 per cent during the last one decade and also showed a decline in recent years. Cotton crop requires irrigation and if the proportion of irrigated area in the country is declining, it means that cotton is increasingly cultivated under rainfed conditions, resulting in yield stagnation. The proportion of cotton area to the gross cropped area (GCA) remained quite stable over the years at slightly above 5 per cent and increased to around 6 per cent during 2010-11 and 2011-12.

Table 3.3: Proportion of Cotton Area to Gross Cropped Area and Proportion of Irrigated Area under Cotton

Years	*Cotton Irrigated Area ('000 Hec)*	*Gross Cropped Area ('000 Hec)*	*Coverage Under Irrigation (%)*	*Proportion of Cotton Area to GCA (%)*
1950-51	482.16	131893	8.2	4.46
1951-52	596.96	133234	9.1	4.92
1952-53	540.60	137675	8.5	4.62
1953-54	587.16	142480	8.4	4.91
1954-55	739.90	144087	9.8	5.24
1955-56	809.00	147311	10	5.49
1956-57	882.20	149492	11	5.36
1957-58	1017.27	145832	12.7	5.49
1958-59	995.00	151629	12.5	5.25
1959-60	941.70	152824	12.9	4.78
1960-61	966.47	152772	12.7	4.98
1961-62	1037.40	156209	13	5.11
1962-63	1089.93	156760	14.1	4.93
1963-64	1257.66	156963	15.3	5.24
1964-65	1297.35	159229	15.5	5.26
1965-66	1265.64	155276	15.9	5.13
1966-67	1262.24	157355	16.1	4.98
1967-68	1336.00	163736	16.7	4.89
1968-69	1254.00	159529	16.5	4.76
1969-70	1267.72	162265	16.4	4.76
1970-71	1316.53	165791	17.3	4.59
1971-72	1583.40	165186	20.3	4.72
1972-73	1612.80	162150	21	4.74
1973-74	1672.97	169872	22.1	4.46
1974-75	1731.24	164191	22.9	4.60
1975-76	1727.25	171296	23.5	4.29
1976-77	1694.94	167334	24.6	4.12
1977-78	2061.94	172232	26.2	4.57
1978-79	2208.64	174802	27.2	4.65
1979-80	2235.75	169589	27.5	4.79
1980-81	2134.86	172630	27.3	4.53
1981-82	2232.62	176750	27.7	4.56
1982-83	2282.30	172748	29	4.56
1983-84	2308.28	179560	29.9	4.30

(Contd.)

Table 3.3: *(Contd.)*

Years	Cotton Irrigated Area ('000 Hec)	Gross Cropped Area ('000 Hec)	Coverage Under Irrigation (%)	Proportion of Cotton Area to GCA (%)
1984-85	2103.30	176330	28.5	4.19
1985-86	2274.06	178464	30.2	4.22
1986-87	2161.45	176405	31.1	3.94
1987-88	2067.20	170738	32	3.78
1988-89	2422.20	182277	33	4.03
1989-90	2629.98	182269	34.2	4.22
1990-91	2447.76	185742	32.9	4.01
1991-92	2550.78	182242	33.3	4.20
1992-93	2608.84	185618	34.6	4.06
1993-94	2540.04	186595	34.7	3.92
1994-95	2691.54	188053	34.2	4.18
1995-96	3164.00	187471	35	4.82
1996-97	3264.96	189502	35.8	4.81
1997-98	3264.16	189988	36.8	4.67
1998-99	3242.21	191649	34.9	4.85
1999-00	3072.96	188396	35.2	4.63
2000-01	2942.94	185340	34.3	4.63
2001-02	2968.20	188286	34	4.64
2002-03	2538.77	175580	33.1	4.37
2003-04	2067.73	190077	27.1	4.01
2004-05	3243.51	191546	36.9	4.59
2005-06	3133.48	193316	36.1	4.49
2006-07	3199.00	192491	35	4.75
2007-08	3345.03	195156	35.1	4.88
2008-09	3375.95	195104	35.88	4.82
2009-10	3424.66	198970	33.22	5.18
2010-11	3473.38	199925	31.18	5.57
2011-12	3522.09	200880	28.89	6.07

Source: Directorate of Economics and Statistics, Ministry of Agriculture & Cooperation, GoI.

Table 3.4: Area under Bt Cotton in India (2002-2010)

Years	Area under cotton (Hec)	Area under Bt cotton (Hec)	Proportion of Area Occupied by Bt cotton (%)	No. of Bt cotton Farmers
2002-03	7670000	50000	0.65	20000
2003-04	7600000	100000	1.32	75000
2004-05	8790000	500000	5.69	350000
2005-06	8680000	1300000	14.98	1000000
2006-07	9140000	3800000	41.58	2300000
2007-08	9410000	6280000	66.74	3800000
2008-09	9410000	7605000	80.82	3880000
2009-10	10310000	8360000	81.09	4629286
2010-11	11000000	9688000	88.08	5378571

Source: Ministry of Agriculture (GoI), ISAAA and Foundation for Biotechnology Awareness and Education.

Table 3.4 shows that the area under Bt cotton in India as a proportion of total cotton area in the country has increased tremendously from less than 1 per cent in 2002-03 to about 88 per cent in 2010-11. The total number of farmers cultivating Bt cotton has also increased by leaps and bounds by more than 200 times within the same period.

Table 3.5: State-wise Adoption of Bt Cotton in India ('000 Hec)

States	*2002-03*	*2003-04*	*2004-05*	*2005-06*	*2006-07*	*2007-08*	*2008-09*	*2009-10*
Maharashtra	25	30	200	607	1840	2880	3130	3396
Andhra Pradesh	8	10	75	280	830	1090	1320	1049
Gujarat	10	36	122	150	470	908	1360	1682
Madhya Pradesh	2	13	80	146	310	500	620	600
Northern Zone*	—	—	—	60	215	682	840	1243
Karnataka	3	4	18	30	85	145	240	273
Tamil Nadu	2	7	5	27	45	70	90	109
Others	—	—	—	—	5	5	5	8
Total	**50**	**100**	**500**	**1300**	**3800**	**6280**	**7605**	**8360**

Source: Ministry of Agriculture (GoI), ISAAA and a Foundation for Biotechnology Awareness and Education.

*Punjab, Haryana, Rajasthan.

Table 3.5 also shows State-wise adoption of Bt cotton area in different States. It would be seen that Maharashtra recorded the highest area, followed by Andhra Pradesh, Gujarat, Madhya Pradesh, Northern Zone, Karnataka and Tamil Nadu. Further, the area under Bt cotton has increased in all the major cultivating States.

It is to be mentioned here that commercial cultivation of Bt cotton had started from 2002-03 only in the States of the central and southern regions of India. In the northern region comprising the States of Punjab, Haryana and Rajasthan, cultivation began from 2005-06 onwards. Hence, in this study the Post-Bt cotton period for the central and southern States have been taken from 2002-03 onwards, while for the northern States, it has been taken from 2005-06 onwards.

It is important to understand here the reason behind the early jump in cotton yields between 2002-03 and 2005-06, despite low adoption of Bt cotton in the early years of its introduction in India. While it is clear that Bt cotton was an engine of productivity growth beginning 2002-03, Gruere & Sun (2012) quoted several studies that reported the prevalent use of unofficial Bt cotton long before its official approval in 2002, especially in the State of Gujarat, which had led India in cotton production during the past decade. Hence the official figures underestimated adoption, especially for the State of Gujarat. But, they also stated that lack of information on adoption rates of these unofficial Bt cotton, was an impediment in understanding the actual contribution of Bt cotton during the period between 2002 and 2005. Their regression results showed that Bt cotton contributed significantly to cotton yield growth, ranging from a 0.29 per cent to 0.39 per cent annual increase in yield for each percentage adoption in each State, or a total increase contribution of 19 per cent over time between 1975 and 2010. But their results also showed that other key factors such as the use of fertilizers, hybrid seeds, human labour, pesticides, and especially the use of irrigation had significant effects on cotton yields. According to T.M. Manjunath of the Foundation for Biotechnology Awareness and Education, at least 50 per cent of increase in cotton yields between 2002 and 2007 could be attributed to Bt technology.

Figure 3.2 shows the State-wise area under cotton. It is seen that over the years, the area under cotton was highest in the State of Maharashtra (above 30 lakh hectares) followed by Gujarat (22 lakh hectares) and Andhra Pradesh (13 lakh hectares). These States were followed by Madhya Pradesh (6 lakh hectares), Punjab and Haryana (5 lakh hectares), Karnataka and Rajasthan (4 lakh hectares) and lastly Tamil Nadu (1 lakh hectare).

Table 3.6: Moving Averages of Area under Cotton (Lakh Hec)

States	*1995-97*	*1997-99*	*1999-01*	*2001-03*	*2003-05*	*2005-07*	*2007-09*	*2009-11*
Punjab	7.40	5.88	5.16	5.00	5.06	5.89	5.56	5.42
Haryana	6.44	5.89	5.70	5.52	5.77	5.32	4.82	5.19
Rajasthan	6.35	6.24	4.80	3.59	4.12	3.91	3.72	4.09
Gujarat	14.84	15.55	16.15	16.58	18.78	22.96	24.67	27.53
Maharashtra	30.98	31.97	31.04	28.50	28.33	30.51	32.80	38.50
Madhya Pradesh	5.27	5.14	5.51	5.86	6.01	6.35	6.20	6.50
Andhra Pradesh	9.87	10.72	10.20	8.80	9.96	10.26	13.38	16.80
Karnataka	6.11	5.55	5.64	4.32	4.05	3.86	4.13	4.47
Tamil Nadu	2.57	2.25	1.93	1.29	1.28	1.24	1.07	1.19
All India	**90.46**	**89.73**	**86.70**	**79.90**	**83.90**	**91.11**	**97.16**	**110.81**

Source: Directorate of Economics and Statistics, Ministry of Agriculture and Cooperation, GoI

Table 3.6 shows moving averages of cotton area, and it is observed that cotton area has increased consistently ever since the introduction of Bt cotton in India in 2002-03, especially in the States of Gujarat, Maharashtra, Andhra Pradesh, Madhya Pradesh and Karnataka.

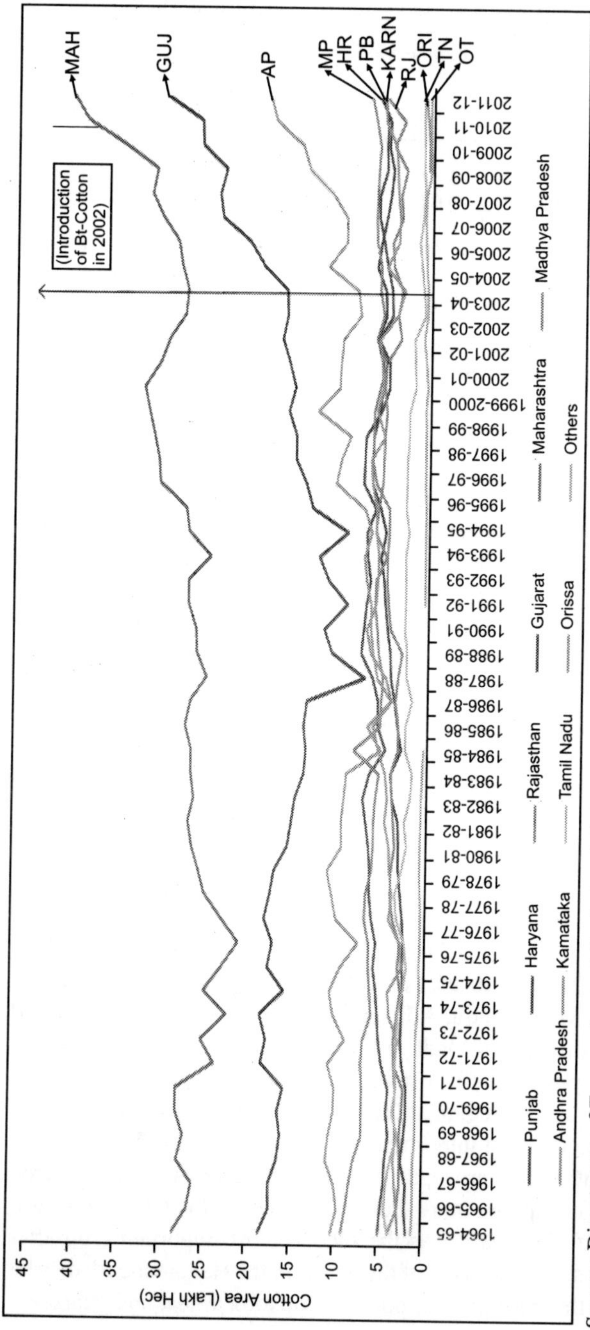

Source: Directorate of Economics and Statistics, Ministry of Agriculture & Cooperation, GOI.

Fig. 3.2: State-wise Area under Cotton (Lakh Hectares).

Table 3.7: Trend Annual Growth Rates of Cotton Area in Various States (%)

States	*Pre-Bt Cotton Period*			*Post-Bt Cotton Period*	*2009 to 2011*
	1970-1979	*1980-1989*	*1990-2001*	*2002-2011*	
Punjab	4.53	0.5	–3.25	–1.33	2.21
Haryana	3.43	3.47	0.74	–0.68	9.24
Rajasthan	4.15	–0.64	–1.44	0.03	9.26
Gujarat	0.23	–5.1	5.24	6.72	7.31
Maharashtra	–0.65	–0.33	1.81	4.49	8.12
Madhya Pradesh	–0.71	–1.24	–0.66	1.87	8.11
Andhra Pradesh	2.15	4.23	5.16	9.45	11.81
Karnataka	0.32	–6.47	–0.40	2.07	13.39
Tamil Nadu	–0.45	1.63	–3.05	4.91	3.02
All India	0.41	–1.22	1.84	4.73	8.64

Source: Directorate of Economics and Statistics, Ministry of Agriculture and Cooperation, GOI.

Table 3.7 shows the trend annual growth rates in cotton area in the Pre and Post-Bt cotton period. In the Pre-Bt cotton period, 3 decades from 1970 to 2001 have been taken. It is seen that the trend growth rates in cotton area have increased in the Post-Bt cotton period from the Pre-Bt cotton period except in the States of Punjab and Haryana, where the growth rates are negative. Further, the last 3 years of available data show that growth rates of cotton area increased significantly in all the States.

The area under cotton as a proportion of gross cropped area in the major cotton growing States between 1995-96 and 2010-11 was highest for Gujarat (20%) followed by Maharashtra (15%), Andhra Pradesh (10%), Haryana and Punjab (7%), Madhya Pradesh (4%), Karnataka (3%), Rajasthan (2%) and Tamil Nadu (1%) (Figure 3.3).

As regards the area under cotton as a proportion of GCA in the major cotton growing districts that have been selected for the study (Figure 3.4), it was seen that Surendranagar district of Gujarat topped the list followed by Yavatmal district of Maharashtra, Adilabad district of Andhra Pradesh and Dhar and Khargone districts of Madhya Pradesh.

Further the cropping pattern in selected districts shows that cotton is a predominant crop in all the regions (Table 3.8). In the Bathinda district of Punjab it was the second most important crop after wheat occupying around 30 per cent of the GCA. In Ferozepur it was the third most important crop after wheat and rice occupying more than 15 per cent of the GCA. In Hissar and Sirsa districts of Haryana it was the second most important crop after wheat occupying around 30 per cent of the GCA. In the Hanumangarh district of Rajasthan, it was the third most important crop after wheat and guarseed

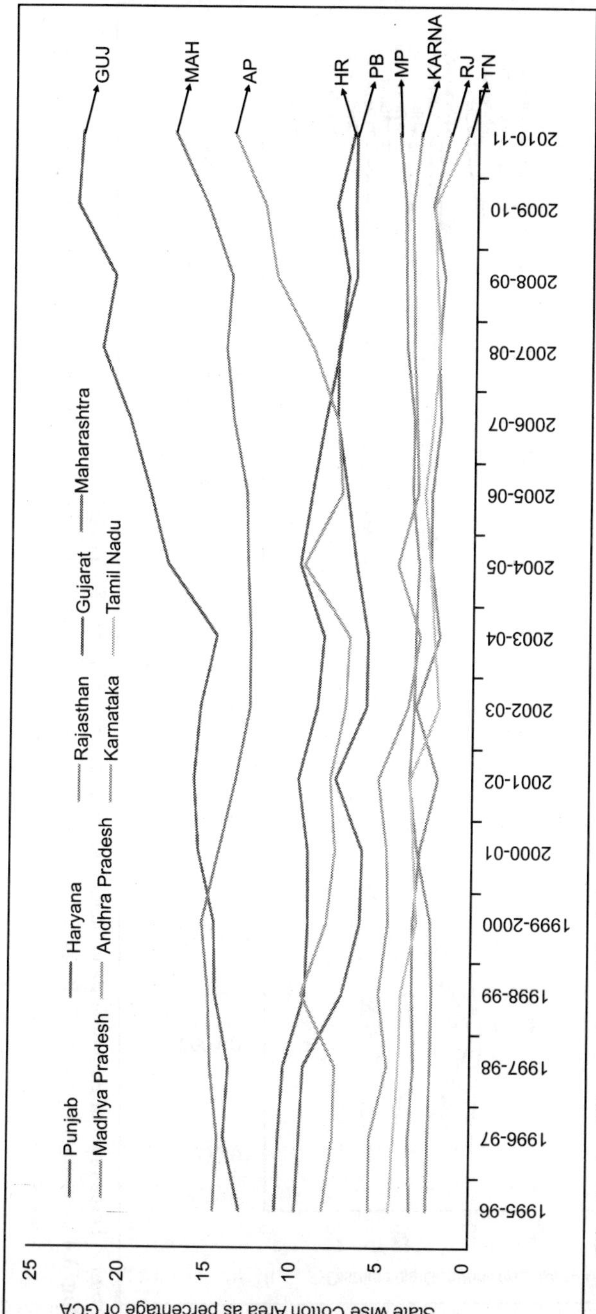

Source: Directorate of Economics and Statistics, Ministry of Agriculture and Cooperation, GoI

Fig. 3.3: Area under Cotton as a Proportion of Gross Cropped Area in the Major Cotton Growing States (%)

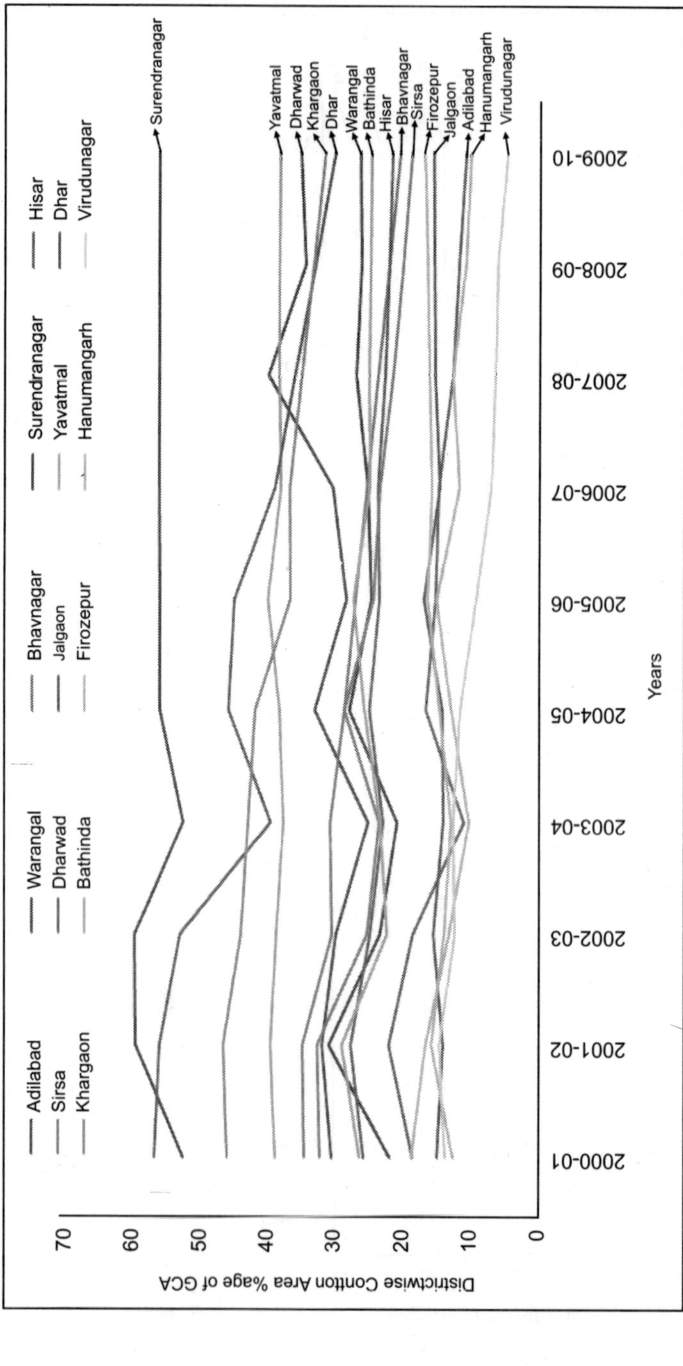

Source: Directorate of Economics and Statistics, Ministry of Agriculture & Cooperation, GoI.

Fig. 3.4: Area under Cotton as a Proportion of Gross Cropped Area in the Major Cotton Growing Districts (%).

occupying around 15 per cent of the GCA. In Gujarat, cotton was the most important crop with the share in Bhavnagar being around 40 per cent and that of Surendranagar being 60 per cent. In Jalgaon and Yavatmal districts of Maharashtra it was the most important crop occupying around 40 per cent of the GCA. In the Dhar district of Madhya Pradesh it was the third most important crop after soyabean and wheat occupying around 15 per cent of the GCA, while in Khargone district it was the most important crop occupying around 30 per cent of the GCA. In the Dharwad district of Karnataka it was the most important crop occupying around 15 per cent of the GCA. In the Adilabad district of Andhra Pradesh it was the most important crop after Wheat occupying around 40 per cent of the GCA. In Warangal it was the most important crop besides rice and maize occupying more than 30 per cent of the GCA. In the Virudunagar district of Tamil Nadu, its position is slowly declining and its area is less than 10 per cent.

The irrigated area under cotton as a proportion of gross irrigated area (GIA) was highest in the State of Gujarat (around 25%). The irrigated area in Gujarat is high because of development of several micro-irrigation systems there. The proportions were relatively less in the other States (Figure 3.5). It was around 10 per cent in the States of Haryana and Punjab. The cotton irrigated area as a proportion of gross irrigated area in the remaining cotton growing States of the central and southern region has been around 5 per cent over the years showing that cotton is being cultivated mainly under rain-fed conditions in the major cotton cultivated areas.

The irrigated area under cotton as a proportion of gross irrigated area in the major cotton growing districts show that the highest proportion of cotton irrigated area was in the district of Surendranagar in Gujarat (around 60%). Bhavnagar district of Gujarat also showed high proportions of irrigated area however its share has declined from 85 to 45 per cent since 2000-01. Khargone district of Madhya Pradesh also showed relatively high shares (above 50%). The proportions were relatively less (less than 40%) in the other districts (Figure 3.6).

Table 3.9 shows moving averages of cotton production, and it is observed that at the all India level, cotton production increased consistently ever since the introduction of Bt cotton in India in 2002-03, especially in the States of Gujarat, Maharashtra, Andhra Pradesh and Karnataka. The highest production was recorded in Gujarat followed by Maharashtra.

Table 3.10 shows the trend annual growth rates in cotton production in the Pre- and Post-Bt cotton period. In the Pre-Bt cotton period, 3 decades from 1970 to 2001 have been taken. It is seen that the trend growth rates in cotton production have shown an increase in the Post-Bt cotton period from the Pre-Bt cotton period excepting in the States of Punjab and Madhya Pradesh,

Table 3.8: Cropping Pattern in Selected Districts (Proportion of Crop Area to GCA (%)

Districts	*Crops*	*2000-01*	*Crops*	*2001-02*	*Crops*	*2002-03*	*Crops*	*2003-04*	*Crops*	*2004-05*
Bathinda	Wheat	48.70	Wheat	49.13	Wheat	47.30	Wheat	47.63	Wheat	47.36
	Colton	29.46	Cotton	32.75	Cotton	24.74	Cotton	25.19	Cotton	27.71
	Rice	19.84	Rice	16.58	Rice	21.18	Rice	20.67	Rice	20.04
Ferozepur	Wheat	49.52	Wheat	49.19	Wheat	48.02	Wheat	49.08	Wheat	48.71
	Rice	32.49	Rice	29.54	Rice	30.45	Rice	31.27	Rice	30.03
	Cotton	14.93	Cotton	18.37	Cotton	15.74	Cotton	14.99	Cotton	16.78
Hissar	Wheat	42.05	Wheat	36.93	Wheat	37.99	Wheat	36.48	Wheat	36.63
	Cotton	28.83	Cotton	31.23	Cotton	27.79	Cotton	25.85	Cotton	27.80
	Bajra	11.78	Bajra	11.88	Bajra	13.75	Bajra	13.18	R&M	12.89
Sirsa	Wheat	44.98	Wheat	41.99	Wheat	39.95	Wheat	43.24	Wheat	41.47
	Cotton	36.83	Cotton	37.42	Cotton	29.00	Cotton	28.91	Cotton	33.21
	Rice	7.34	R&M	8.83	R&M	17.13	R&M	11.93	R&M	13.49
Hanumangarh	Wheat	32.96	Guar seed	22.07	R&M	40.45	Gram	26.37	Wheat	41.7
	Cotton	26.82	Wheat	19.23	Wheat	20.92	Wheat	20.28	Gram	20.3
	Gram	12.56	Cotton	16.94	Cotton	14.78	Cotton	13.30	Bajra	18.3
Bhavnagar	Cotton	35.94	Cotton	35.17	Groundnut	36.96	Cotton	35.7	Cotton	40.96
	Groundnut	28.02	Groundnut	34.25	Cotton	30.42	Groundnut	33.0	Groundnut	29.05
	Bajra	18.49	Bajra	14.55	Bajra	13.32	Bajra	13.1	Bajra	13.46
Surendranagar	Cotton	64.93	Cotton	67.10	Cotton	64.28	Cotton	57.85	Cotton	61.99
	Sesamum	13.50	Sesamum	13.00	Sesamum	13.45	Sesamum	17.14	Sesamum	15.46
	Bajra	11.51	Bajra	11.23	Bajra	11.29	Bajra	12.55	Bajra	9.94
Jalgaon	Cotton	45.88	Cotton	45.41	Cotton	42.54	Cotton	39.75	Cotton	42.99
	Jowar	18.95	Jowar	19.48	Jowar	20.76	Jowar	19.57	Jowar	18.65
	Bajra	7.11	Bajra	7.04	Urad	7.53	Urad	6.76	Urad	6.49
Yavatmal	Cotton	46.8	Cotton	47.17	Cotton	45.05	Cotton	41.79	Cotton	39.92
	Jowar	16.15	Jowar	15.72	Jowar	15.58	Jowar	18.05	Soyabean	21.15
	Arhar	12.49	Arhar	13.28	Arhar	14.22	Arhar	14.47	Arhar	15.25
Dhar	Soyabean	47.09	Soyabean	36.51	Soyabean	34.04	Soyabean	32.85	Soyabean	43.63
	Cotton	15.64	Wheat	18.13	Turmeric	13.93	Wheat	22.87	Wheat	3.53
	Maize	13.33	Cotton	14.62	Cotton	13.93	Cotton	14.24	Maize	13.09
Khargone	Cotton	39.56	Cotton	40.47	Turmeric	28.24	Cotton	37.68	Jowar	29.81
	Jowar	18.56	Jowar	18.69	Cotton	28.24	Jowar	16.38	Wheat	22.48
	Soyabean	12.04	Soyabean	10.59	Jowar	12.74	Wheat	11.81	Soyabean	21.48
Dharwad	Cotton	18.91	Cotton	22.84	Cotton	19.11	Jovar	16.11	Cotton	16.90
	Dry chillies	13.09	Dry chillies	14.30	Dry chillles	11.84	Gram	12.07	Jowar	11.30
	Jowar	11.43	Jowar	12.45	Jowar	11.29	Wheat	11.54	Dry chillies	11.28
Adilabad	Cotton	31.46	Cotton	33.06	Cotton	30.28	Cotton	25.71	Cotton	33.51
	Jowar	22.48	Jowar	20.96	Jowar	17.20	Jowar	17.55	Jowar	17.55
	Rice	14.40	Rice	14.53	Rice	14.39	Rice	14.36	Soyabean	10.96
Warangal	Rice	35.67	Cotton	31.32	Rice	27.22	Rice	29.30	Cotton	28.49
	Cotton	22.28	Rice	30.81	Cotton	24.00	Cotton	21.37	Rice	24.26
	Maize	9.95	Groundnut	7.78	Maize	13.51	Maize	14.65	Maize	13.38
Virudunagar	Rice	24.39	Rice	31.77	Rice	25.48	Rice	19.94	Rice	28.49
	Cotton	17.80	Cotton	22.98	Cotton	14.46	Cotton	14.77	Jowar	11.12
	Jowar	9.10	Moong	7.75	Moong	8.01	Moong	9.84	Moong	9.51
	Maize	8.69	Jowar	7.57	Maize	7.17	Coconut	7.08	Coconut	8.13
	Bajra	7.87	Bajra	6.94	Coconut	6.86	Groundnut	7.07	Maize	7.90
	Groundnut	7.49	Groundnut	6.23	Groundnut	5.70	Maize	6.96	Groundnut	7.18

(Contd.)

Table 3.8: (*Contd.*)

Districts	*Crops*	*2005-06*	*Crops*	*2006-07*	*Crops*	*2007-08*	*Crops*	*2008-09*	*Crops*	*2009-10*
Bathinda	Wheat	47.72								
	Cotton	29.65								
	Rice	18.66								
Ferozepur	Wheat	48.67								
	Rice	29.76								
	Cotton	17.65								
Hissar										
Sirsa										
Hanumangarh			Wheat	27.84	Guar seed	26.33	Guar seed	30.54	Wheat	21.96
			Gram	22.33	Gram	18.96	Wheat	17.06	Guar seed	19.79
			R&M	20.88	Wheat	17.80	Gram	16.49	Cotton	17.66
Bhavnagar										
Surendranagar										
Jalgaon	Cotton	69.1	Cotton	42.82						
	Bajra	10.6	Jowar	16.66						
	Gram	8.4	Gram	6.01						
Yavatmal	Cotton	54.34	Cotton	41.1						
	Soyabean	35.64	Soyabean	26.6						
	Gram	6.19	Arhar	11.3						
Dhar					Soyabean	33.71				
					Wheat	29.13				
					Cotton	15.71				
Khargone					Cotton	43.36				
					Wheat	15.65				
					Jowar	14.00				
Dharwad			Cotton	15.04	Cotton	14.08				
			Dry chilies	10.04	Jowar	9.92				
			Gram	9.34	Dry chillies	9.51				
Adilabad	Cotton	28.85	Cotton	31.22	Cotton	40.71			Cotton	46.43
	Jowar	14.76	Soyabean	14.18	Soyabean	11.29			Soyabean	15.24
	Rice	14.25	Jowar	13.47	Jowar	10.23			Jowar	9.65
Warangal	Rice	33.70	Rice	35.22	Rice	32.4S			Cotton	34.49
	Cotton	25.25	Cotton	25.90	Cotton	27.79			Rice	23.16
	Maize	13.03	Maize	12.74	Maize	13.72			Maize	12.77
Virudunagar	Rice	24.44	Rice	27.24	Rice	24.09	Rice	26.98		
	Cotton	11.01	Maize	11.06	Maize	11.31	Maize	13.67		
	Moong	9.05	Cotton	9.60	Moong	8.90	Jowar	9.20		
	Maize	8.88	Moong	S.21	Jowar	7.92	Coconut	7.32		
	Jowar	7.80	Coconut	7.33	Coconut	7.59	Groundnut	7.30		
	Groundnut	7.45	Groundnut	5.99	Cotton	7.45	Cotton	7.23		

Source: Directorate of Economics and Statistics, Ministry of Agriculture & Cooperation, GoI.

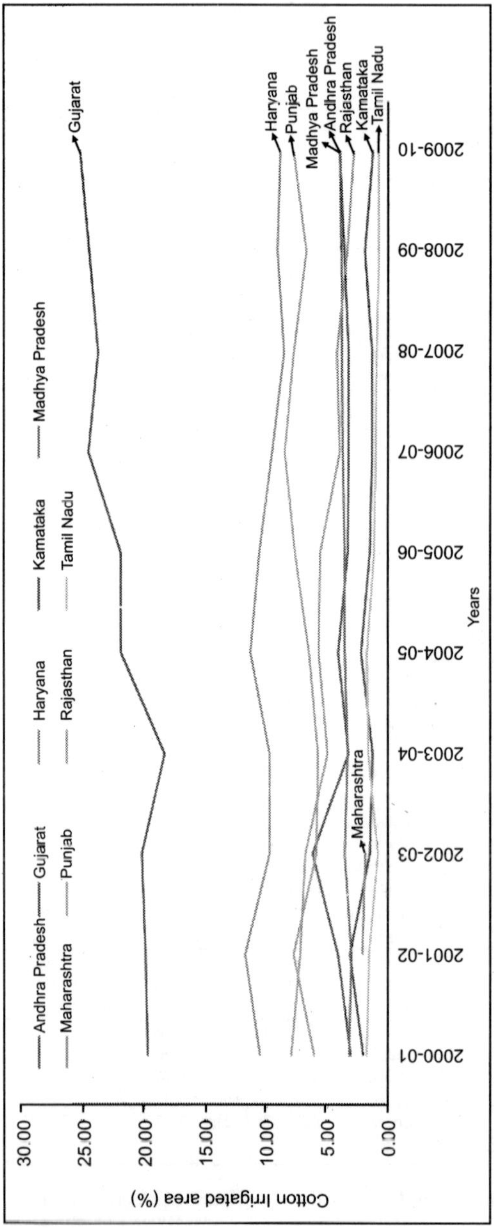

Source: Directorate of Economics and Statistics, Ministry of Agriculture & Cooperation, GoI.

Fig. 3.5: Irrigated Area under Cotton as a Proportion of Gross Irrigated Area in the Major Cotton Growing States (%).

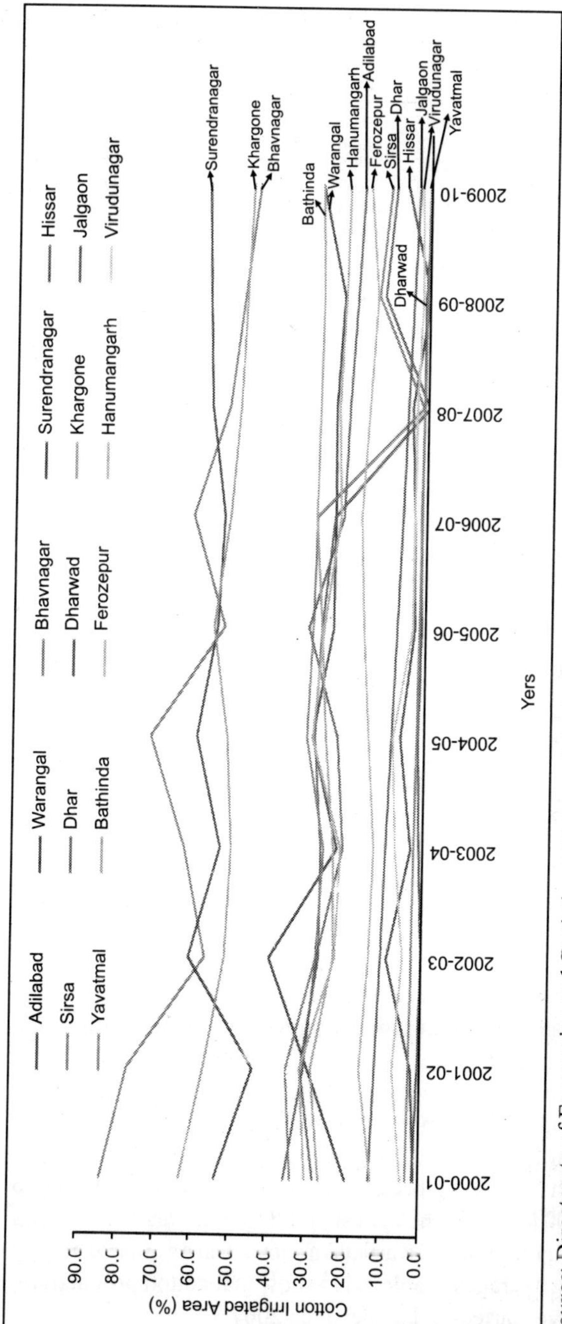

Source: Directorate of Economics and Statistics, Ministry of Agriculture & Cooperation, GoI.

Fig. 3.6: Irrigated Area under Cotton as a Proportion of Gross Irrigated Area in the Major Cotton Growing Districts (%).

Table 3.9: Moving Averages of Production of Cotton (Lakh Bales)

States	1995-97	1997-99	1999-01	2001-03	2003-05	2005-07	2007-09	2009-11
Punjab	12.62	6.78	8.87	9.03	15.95	22.33	16.83	15.33
Haryana	11.27	8.90	8.73	8.58	13.67	15.00	14.75	15.42
Rajasthan	13.08	12.00	10.27	7.05	10.38	9.33	9.50	12.33
Gujarat	35.83	39.00	27.93	37.67	70.67	100.00	99.33	105.00
Maharashtra	27.42	28.33	30.20	30.43	39.67	50.00	63.25	72.25
Madhya Pradesh	18.67	19.08	18.27	19.22	17.88	18.67	17.75	16.42
Andhra Pradesh	26.22	24.10	24.87	24.67	29.97	37.00	51.17	51.83
Karnataka	8.67	7.75	7.25	5.40	6.23	6.83	9.75	11.42
Tamil Nadu	5.33	5.50	5.33	3.92	4.92	4.83	4.67	5.00
Total	**163.67**	**159.67**	**151.33**	**157.67**	**222.00**	**277.00**	**300.67**	**329.73**

Source: Directorate of Economics and Statistics, Ministry of Agriculture and Cooperation, GoI.

Table 3.10: Trend Annual Growth Rates of Cotton Production in Various States (%)

States	Pre-Bt cotton Period			Post-Bt cotton Period	2009-10 to 2011-12
	1970-1979	1980-1989	1990-2001	2002-2011	
Punjab	4.11	9.54	–5.53	–7.01	14.35
Haryana	4.58	2.20	–1.80	1.19	5.58
Rajasthan	7.70	4.18	–1.90	6.06	15.47
Gujarat	1.39	–6.70	7.24	11.88	7.85
Maharashtra	8.44	2.86	6.52	11.91	2.44
Madhya Pradesh	0.24	1.98	6.31	–1.00	5.58
Andhra Pradesh	14.66	–1.05	2.90	10.96	–6.15
Karnataka	6.62	5.70	–2.24	11.09	–1.03
Tamil Nadu	3.49	7.36	0.04	3.47	0.00
All India	4.39	2.83	2.72	9.25	6.37

Source: Directorate of Economics and Statistics, Ministry of Agriculture and Cooperation, GoI.

where the growth rates were negative. However, the last 3 years of available data show that growth rates in Cotton production reduced significantly in the central and southern States.

From Figure 3.7 it is seen that cotton lint yields have shown increasing trends in all the cotton cultivating States. Over the last three years the highest yielding States were Tamil Nadu (714.29 kg/hec) followed by Gujarat (648.46 kg/hec), Andhra Pradesh (524.40 kg/hec), Rajasthan (512.21 kg/hec), Punjab and Haryana (around 500 kg/hec). The lowest yielding state was Maharashtra (319.03 kg/hec). Madhya Pradesh and Karnataka showed an average of around 420 kg/hec. The moving averages (Table 3.11) show that cotton productivity in most of the States have started to decline since 2007.

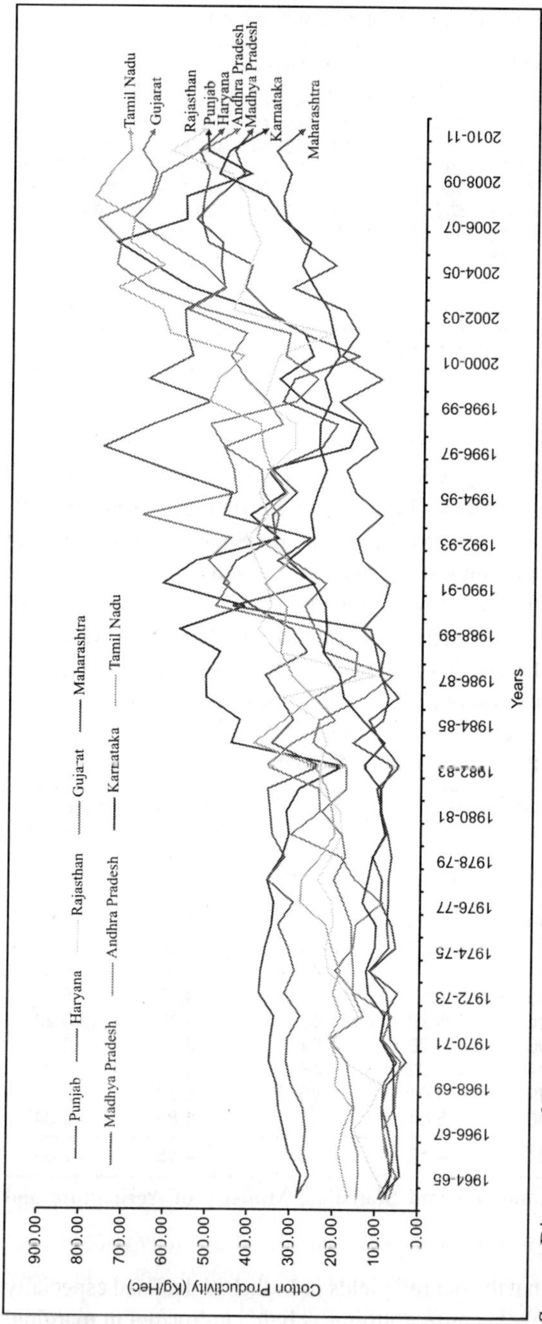

Source: Directorate of Economics and Statistics, Ministry of Agriculture and Cooperation, GoI.

Fig. 3.7: State-wise Cotton Productivity (Kg Lint/Hec).

Table 3.11: Moving Averages of Cotton Productivity (kg/hec)

States	1995-97	1997-99	1999-01	2001-03	2003-05	2005-07	2007-09	2009-11
Punjab	289.97	196.12	291.93	306.93	535.87	644.23	515.00	480.93
Haryana	297.26	257.02	260.32	264.50	402.89	479.32	520.23	504.98
Rajasthan	350.26	326.75	363.61	333.84	428.44	405.80	434.53	512.21
Gujarat	410.40	426.37	294.10	386.21	639.80	740.31	684.50	648.46
Maharashtra	150.45	150.65	165.42	181.53	238.03	278.57	327.82	319.03
Madhya Pradesh	602.15	630.75	563.24	557.16	506.13	500.00	486.96	429.36
Andhra Pradesh	451.40	382.30	414.31	476.52	511.65	613.26	649.94	524.40
Karnataka	241.13	237.24	218.66	212.34	261.65	300.69	401.66	433.87
Tamil Nadu	352.33	415.56	470.59	514.82	652.99	660.86	739.13	714.29
All India	**307.58**	**302.49**	**296.73**	**335.46**	**449.82**	**516.83**	**526.06**	**505.86**

Source: Directorate of Economics and Statistics, Ministry of Agriculture and Cooperation, GoI.

Table 3.12 shows the trend growth rates in cotton productivity in the Pre and Post-Bt cotton period. Just like in the case of cotton production, the trend growth rates in cotton productivity have shown an increase in the Post-Bt cotton period from the Pre-Bt cotton period in all the States excepting Punjab and Madhya Pradesh, where the growth rates are negative. The growth rates during the decade of Bt cotton cultivation have increased significantly in all the States and are highest in the States of Karnataka, Maharashtra, Rajasthan and Gujarat. However, the last 3 years of available data show that growth rates in cotton productivity where reduced in various States except Punjab.

Table 3.12: Trend Growth Rates of Cotton Productivity in Various States (%)

States	Pre-Bt Cotton Period			Post-Bt Cotton Period	2009-10 to 2011-12
	1970-79	1980-89	1990-01	2002-11	
Punjab	–0.40	9.00	–2.35	–5.76	11.88
Haryana	1.11	–1.23	–2.52	1.88	–3.35
Rajasthan	3.41	4.85	–0.46	6.03	5.69
Gujarat	1.15	–1.69	1.90	4.83	0.50
Maharashtra	9.15	3.20	4.62	7.10	–5.25
Madhya Pradesh	0.96	3.26	7.01	–2.82	–2.34
Andhra Pradesh	12.24	–5.07	–2.16	1.37	–16.07
Karnataka	6.29	13.01	–1.85	8.83	–12.71
Tamil Nadu	3.96	5.64	3.18	1.89	–2.94
All India	3.96	4.10	0.86	4.15	–2.09

Source: Directorate of Economics and Statistics, Ministry of Agriculture and Cooperation, GoI.

It was stated earlier that the overall yields in India had declined especially in the last 3 years probably because cotton was being cultivated in marginal lands. It is found from Figures 3.2 and 3.7 that over the last 3 years, especially from 2009-10 onwards, the average cotton area was the highest in the States of Maharashtra (38 lakh hectares), followed by Gujarat (27.6 lakh hectares), Andhra Pradesh (17.07 lakh hectares). However, these States, especially Maharashtra, have not shown commensurate high productivity of cotton during the last 3 years. The highest average yields of cotton over the last 3 years were seen in Tamil Nadu (714.29 kg/hec) whose average area under cotton was only 1.19 lakh hectares. Tamil Nadu was followed by Gujarat (648.46 kg/hec) and Andhra Pradesh (524.40 kg/hec), that showed relatively higher area (above 20 lakh hectares). These States were followed by Rajasthan (512.21 kg/hec), Haryana (505 kg/hec) and Punjab (480 kg/hec), whose cotton area was around 5 lakh hectares. The yield in Maharashtra, the highest ranking state in terms of cotton area, was the lowest (319.42 kg/hec). The cotton area in Madhya Pradesh was 6.53 lakh hectares but its corresponding yield was just 430 kg/hec. Some pockets in Maharashtra and Madhya Pradesh are mainly rain-fed with shallow soils and erratic rainfall patterns and without much irrigation. Hence, these can be termed 'marginal lands' compared to other traditional cotton growing areas in the States. Further the yields in these states have also shown a decline despite area increases.

Trends in Cotton Prices

As regards cotton prices (Table 3.13) it is seen that average Minimum Support Prices (MSP) of cotton was ₹ 1775/Qtl in 2002-03 that increased to ₹ 3050 per qtl in 2011-12. The MSP of cotton have increased throughout, but the fluctuations in cotton prices measured through coefficient of variation are seen to be quite high at above 20 per cent in both the Pre as well as Post-Bt cotton period.

It is now important to understand State-wise trends in farm harvest prices (FHP) of cotton. The farm harvest price (FHP) of any commodity is defined as the price at which the commodity is disposed of by the producer to the trader at the farm or village site during specified harvest period. In this context it is seen from Figure 3.8 that farm harvest prices have been showing an upward trend over the years, with high growth rates in the Post-Bt cotton period in all States. The prices are seen to be highest in the State of Punjab (₹ 4500/qtl). The increase in cotton production in recent years could also be attributed to increase in the support as well as market prices. Furthermore, the coefficient of variation in farm harvest prices (Table 3.13) in the Post-Bt cotton period are much greater than those in the Pre-Bt cotton period indicating high instability in farm harvest prices across different States.

Table 3.13: Minimum Support Prices of Cotton (₹ /Qtl)

Years	*MSP of Cotton of Medium Staple Length (Rs/Qtl)*	*MSP of Cotton of Long Staple Length (Rs/Qtl)*	*Cotton MSP (Rs/Qtl)*	*Coefficient of Variation (%)*
1992-1993	800	950	875	Pre-Bt Cotton Period CV = 23.37%
1993-1994	900	1050	975	
1994-1995	1000	1200	1100	
1995-1996	1150	1350	1250	
1996-1997	1180	1380	1280	
1997-1998	1330	1530	1430	
1998-1999	1440	1650	1545	
1999-2000	1575	1775	1675	
2000-2001	1625	1825	1725	
2001-2002	1675	1875	1775	
2002-2003	1675	1875	1775	
2003-2004	1725	1925	1825	Post-Bt Cotton Period CV = 22.74%
2004-2005	1760	1960	1860	
2005-2006	1760	1980	1870	
2006-2007	1770	1990	1880	
2007-2008	1800	2030	1915	
2008-2009	2500	3000	2750	
2009-2010	2500	3000	2750	
2010-2011	2500	3000	2750	
2011-2012	2800	3300	3050	

Source: Directorate of Economics and Statistics, Ministry of Agriculture and Cooperation, GoI.

Table 3.14: State-wise Coefficient of Variation of Farm Harvest Prices of Cotton (%)

States	*Pre-Bt Cotton Period (1998-99 to 2001-02)*		*Post-Bt Cotton Period (2002-03 to 2009-10)*	
	Trend Growth Rates (%)	*CV (%)*	*Trend Growth Rates (%)*	*CV (%)*
Andhra Pradesh	–2.81	8.66	5.16	19.36
Gujarat	–1.58	6.96	6.28	21.08
Haryana	–0.92	5.88	7.71	11.75
Karnataka	0.27	18.64	6.68	22.99
Madhya Pradesh	–4.84	9.30	5.31	18.00
Maharashtra	8.66	12.89	4.10	13.12
Punjab	3.37	8.68	19.67	40.87
Rajasthan	1.52	8.49	18.11	28.02
Tamil Nadu	–3.19	5.18	–1.90	8.40

Source: Directorate of Economics and Statistics, Ministry of Agriculture and Cooperation, GoI.

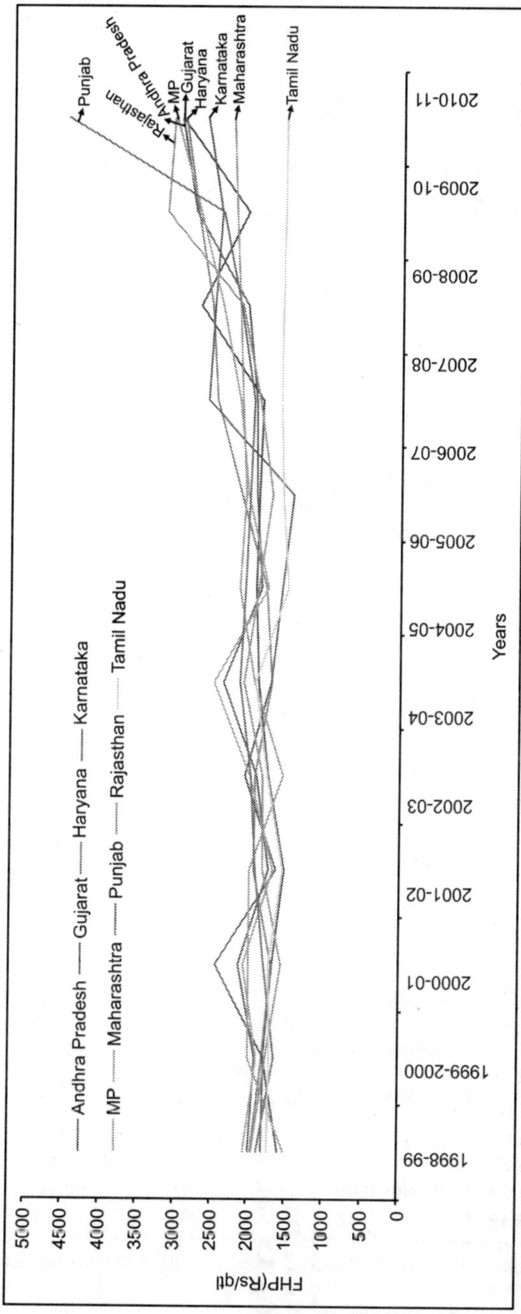

Source: Directorate of Economics and Statistics, Ministry of Agriculture and Cooperation, GoI.

Fig. 3.8: Farm Harvest Prices of Cotton (Rs./qtl)

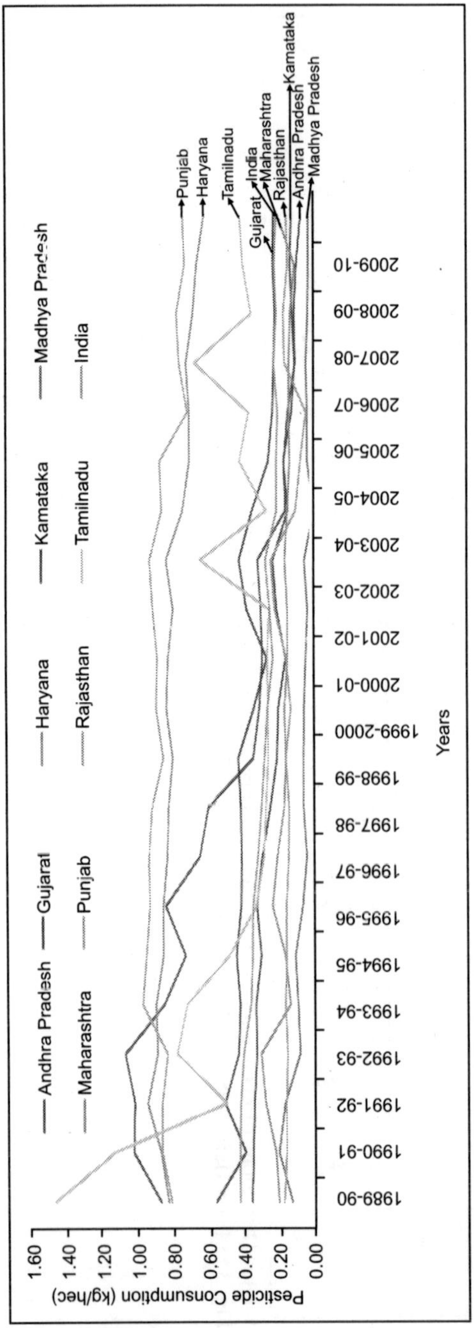

Source: Directorate of Economics and Statistics, Ministry of Agriculture and Cooperation, GoI.

Fig. 3.9: State-wise Consumption of Pesticides in India (kg/hec)

Pesticide Usage in Cotton

According to the Ministry of Chemicals and Petrochemicals in India, cotton accounts for the maximum share of pesticide consumption i.e. around 37 per cent followed by rice (20%). Together they account for around 57 per cent of the total pesticide consumption. As a result pesticide consumption is largely driven by the production trend in these two crops. According to **Gandhi and Namboodiri (2006)**, by the year 2006-07 about 96,000 metric tonnes of technical grade pesticides were being produced in the country of which 54 per cent were consumed on Cotton.

From Figure 3.9 it is seen that the highest pesticide consumption in India are in the States of Punjab and Haryana (0.85 kg/hec). The consumption in Andhra Pradesh was highest during the decade of the 90s (more than 1 kg/hec), but has shown a sharp decline in recent years. The State of Tamil Nadu has also shown an increase in pesticide consumption in recent years (above 0.6 kg/hec). The consumption of pesticides has shown a declining trend in the Post-Bt cotton period.

From Table 3.15 showing average per hectare pesticide consumption in India, it is seen that pesticide consumption reduced from 0.28 kg/hec in the Pre-Bt cotton period between 1996-97 to 2001-02 to 0.22 kg/hec in the Post-Bt cotton period between 2002-03 to 2009-10, a decline of 23.45 per cent. Further the growth rates of pesticide consumption declined at a slow rate in the Post-Bt cotton period (–1.67%) as compared to the Pre-Bt cotton period (–5.63%). A decline in pesticide use growth rates was seen in all the States

Table 3.15: Pesticide Consumption in India

States	*Pre-Bt Cotton Period (1996-97 to 2001-02)*		*Post-Bt Cotton Period (2002-03 to 2009-10)*		*Average (kg/hec) 2007-08 to 2009-10*
	Average (kg/hec)	*Growth Rates (%)*	*Average (kg/hec)*	*Growth Rates (%)*	
Andhra Pradesh	0.42	–15.93	0.15	–15.47	0.10
Gujarat	0.38	–5.32	0.27	–8.02	0.23
Karnataka	0.22	–8.11	0.15	–6.63	0.13
Madhya Pradesh	0.05	–5.10	0.04	9.71	0.03
Maharashtra	0.17	–5.69	0.15	–0.38	0.15
Haryana	0.80	–1.55	0.68	–3.33	0.65
Punjab	0.89	–0.45	0.74	0.23	0.75
Rajasthan	0.15	–3.59	0.14	25.38	0.16
Tamil Nadu	0.27	–2.18	0.44	–1.21	0.39
India	0.28	–5.63	0.22	–1.67	0.22

Source: Directorate of Economics and Statistics, Ministry of Agriculture and Cooperation, GoI.

except Madhya Pradesh, Punjab and Rajasthan, where they increased. Minimal change was observed in the latest years of available data between 2007-08 and 2009-10.

Table 3.16: Moving Averages of Pesticide Consumption in India (kg/hec)

States	*1995-97*	*1997-99*	*1999-01*	*2001-03*	*2003-05*	*2005-07*	*2007-09*	*2009-11*
Andhra Pradesh	0.70	0.42	0.30	0.26	0.16	0.12	0.10	0.08
Gujarat	0.42	0.40	0.33	0.39	0.28	0.23	0.23	0.23
Karnataka	0.29	0.22	0.19	0.20	0.15	0.12	0.13	0.13
Madhya Pradesh	0.06	0.06	0.05	0.03	0.03	0.04	0.03	0.03
Maharashtra	0.21	0.17	0.16	0.16	0.14	0.14	0.15	0.20
Haryana	0.83	0.82	0.82	0.79	0.72	0.70	0.65	0.62
Punjab	0.92	0.88	0.89	0.90	0.81	0.75	0.75	0.74
Rajasthan	0.15	0.15	0.17	0.19	0.08	0.13	0.16	0.15
Tamil Nadu	0.30	0.27	0.26	0.39	0.35	0.46	0.39	0.42
All India	**0.32**	**0.28**	**0.25**	**0.25**	**0.21**	**0.21**	**0.22**	**0.21**

Source: Directorate of Economics and Statistics, Ministry of Agriculture and Cooperation, GoI.

At the all India level, moving averages of pesticide consumption (Table 3.16) show a decline and stagnation in its consumption ever since 2001-2003. This is the situation in all the States, except Maharashtra, Rajasthan and Tamil Nadu, where pesticide consumption levels have started to increase in recent years.

Further, from Figure 3.10 it is seen that the proportion of insecticide cost to the total cost of cotton has plummeted in the State of Punjab, while the other States have shown some decline, though it is increasing gradually in the last two years. From Figures 3.9 and 3.10 and Tables 3.15 and 3.16 it is seen that, the total consumption of pesticide, as well as proportion of insecticide cost to total cost of cotton cultivation in the cotton growing States have shown a declining trend in the Post-Bt cotton period as a whole, but it has shown a slight increase in recent years. Further, the growth rates of pesticide consumption declined at a slow rate in the Post-Bt cotton period compared to the Pre-Bt cotton period. Therefore the decline in cotton yields in recent years can to some extent be attributed to increased attacks by sucking pests not controlled by the current Bt technologies.

During the field survey farmers reported that with the introduction of Bt cotton, though Bollworm damage had declined, there was an increased damage of sucking pests such as Jassids, White flies, Thrips, Mealy bugs and bacterial, fungal and viral diseases. As a consequence insecticide usage was increasing gradually. Further, it is to be mentioned that the first generation Bt cotton (BG I) that was used for commercial cultivation since 2002-03, had over the

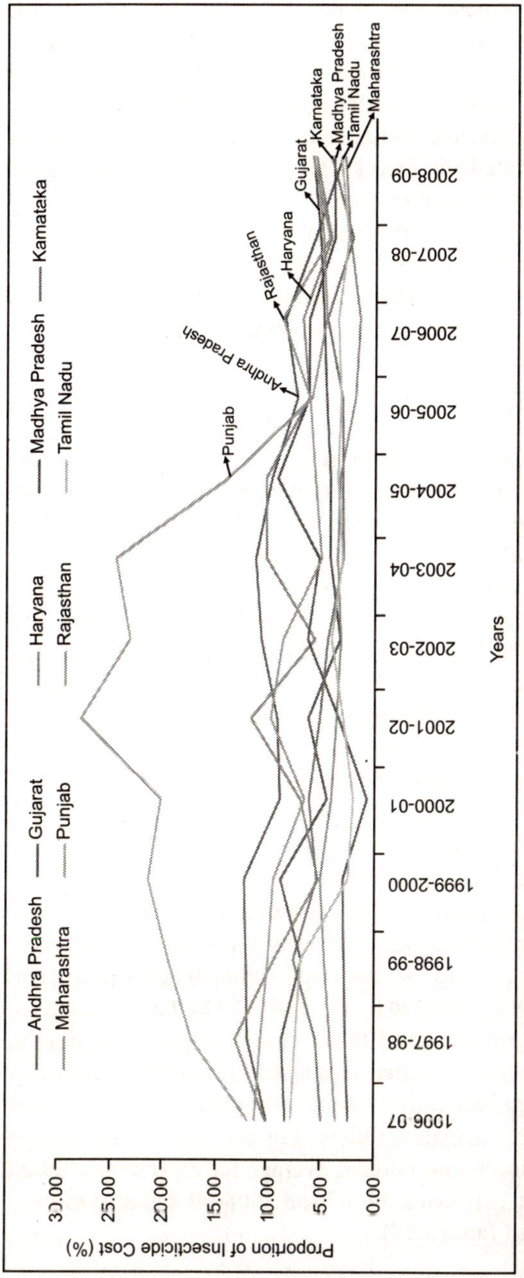

Source: Directorate of Economics and Statistics, Ministry of Agriculture and Cooperation, GoI.

Fig. 3.10: State-wise Proportion of Insecticide Cost to Total Cost of Cotton (%)

years, started to develop resistance to certain types of pests, thereby necessitating the use of more pesticides. Hence the growth rates of pesticide consumption declined slowly at a trend growth rate of –1.67 per cent in the Post-Bt cotton period. Herein it is important to point out that a CICR report of 2001 stated that seed varietal proliferation was a major menace in maintaining purity, arresting pest load and extending technologies. The multiple varietal scenarios complicated the insect pest problems and also created problems in the production of adequate quantities of good quality seeds. It will be seen from Chapter 5 that, seed companies in India manufacture and market over a 1000 Bt hybrid seeds that are being used by farmers in different regions. As the CICR report states, such huge proliferation of seeds will result in complicated insect pest problems, that would affect cotton yields.

Fertilizer Usage in Cotton

In the year 2003-04, cotton occupied an area of 8 million hectares and accounted for 6.0 per cent (1.01 million tonnes) of total fertilizer consumption (FAO). Fertilizer use on irrigated cotton (153.5 kg/ha) was higher than on rain-fed cotton (97.7 kg/ha). The shares of irrigated and rainfed cotton in total fertilizer consumption were 2.7 and 3.3 per cent, respectively. The average per hectare use of fertilizer on cotton was 116.8 kg (89.5 kg/ha N, 22.6 kg/ha P_2O_5 and 4.8 kg/ha K_2O). The maximum load was found in the central region that accounted for 54 per cent of the total fertilizer consumption in cotton. About 45 per cent of the total fertilizer used in cotton was consumed in irrigated cotton growing area and 55 per cent consumed in rainfed area (FAO).

From Figure 3.11 it is seen that per hectare fertilizer consumption in cotton is on the rise, especially since 2007-08. The average consumption of fertilizers has increased from 95 kg/hec in the Pre-Bt cotton period to 120 kg/hec in the Post Bt-cotton period, an increase of 26.72 per cent. In the year 2008-09, the highest amount of fertilizer consumption in the cotton crop was found in the southern region (227 kg/hec) led by Tamil Nadu (308 kg/hec) followed by the northern region (151 kg/hec) led by Punjab (185 kg/hec) and then the central region (138 kg/hec) led by Gujarat (177 kg/hec). During the Pre-Bt cotton period, the growth rate of fertilizer consumption in cotton in the country was –1.54 per cent which increased to 8.52 per cent in the Post-Bt cotton period. The highest growth rates in the Post-Bt cotton period was seen in the northern States (mainly irrigated) followed by the southern and central (rainfed States) in close succession. Further, average fertilizer consumption in the latest years available, between 2006-07 and 2008-09, has also showed an increase in all the States (Table 3.17).

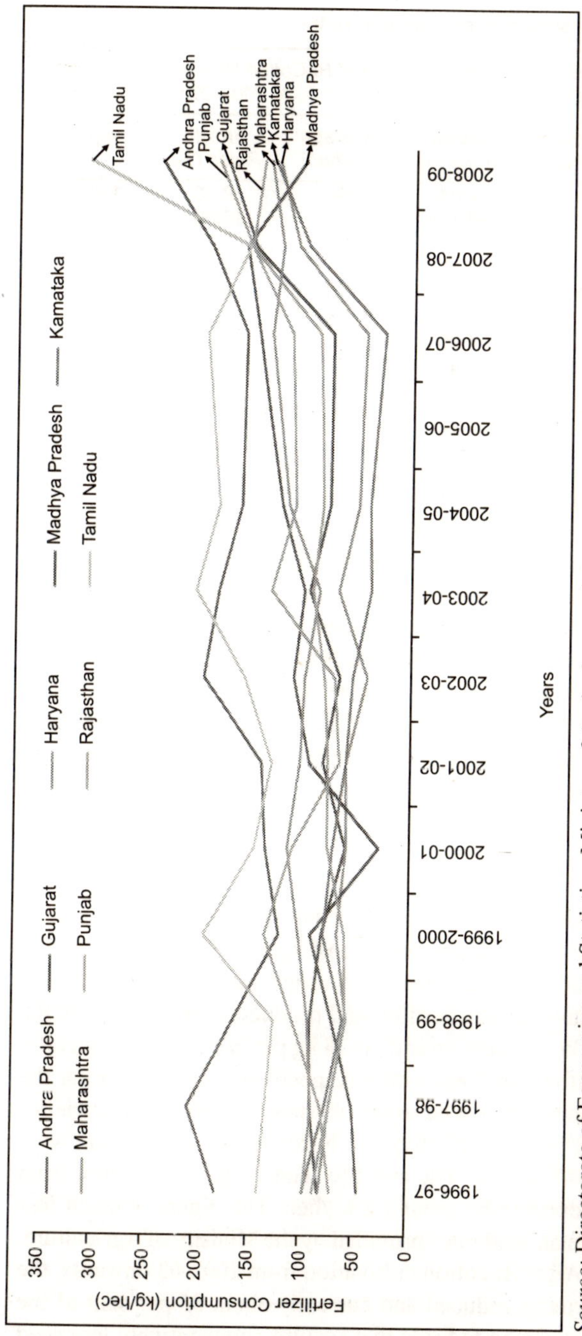

Source: Directorate of Economics and Statistics, Ministry of Agriculture and Cooperation, GoI.

Fig. 3.11: Fertilizer Consumption in Cotton (kg/hec)

Table 3.17: Fertilizer Consumption of Cotton in India

States	*Pre-Bt Cotton Period (1996-97 to 2001-02)*		*Post-Bt Cotton Period (2002-03 to 2008-09)*		*Average (kg/hec) 2006-07 to 2008-09*
	Average (kg/hec)	*Growth Rates (%)*	*Average (kg/hec)*	*Growth Rates (%)*	
Andhra Pradesh	158	–7.84	184	2.50	196
Karnataka	74	–6.31	60	16.09	85
Tamil Nadu	144	1.03	198	5.71	219
Gujarat	81	–3.99	102	14.74	134
Maharashtra	100	3.57	116	6.69	130
Madhya Pradesh	63	6.32	124	3.28	135
Haryana	61	–4.90	81	48.76	93
Punjab	76	2.42	127	33.95	141
Rajasthan	98	2.71	130	10.92	136
India	95	–1.54	120	8.52	141

Source: Directorate of Economics and Statistics, Ministry of Agriculture and Cooperation, GoI.

The proportion of fertilizer cost to total cost of cotton has shown fluctuations in all the major cotton cultivating States within the range of 4 to 10 per cent. Overall the proportions are showing increasing trends in the Post-Bt cotton period. The State of Madhya Pradesh has shown the highest fluctuation. Fertilizer cost as a proportion of cost of cultivation declined slightly only in Rajasthan and Madhya Pradesh, while in the rest of the States it increased (Figure 3.12). The increase was due to increase in fertilizer prices as well as increased use of fertilisers.

Seed Usage in Cotton

It is observed from Table 3.18 that the total seed usage of cotton has declined from 9.23 kg/hec in the Pre-Bt cotton period to 6 kg/hec in the Post Bt-cotton period. It is to be mentioned here that, seed usage varies according to the variety, its growth behaviour, soil fertility and production practices (CICR). Seed usage of 15 to 25 kg per hectare and 10-18 kg per hectare were generally used for American cotton and Desi cotton respectively. Further, during the field survey it was reported that seed usage of some Non-Bt cotton varieties such as Y1, 846, 1378 cultivated before the introduction of Bt cotton were high ranging from 12-17 kg/hec. The average seed usage in Bt cotton from the field survey was found to be around 2 kg/hec. This figure is much less then the time series data on seed rates provided by the Ministry of Agriculture, Government of India. After Bt cotton cultivation from 2002-03 onwards, the number of Non-Bt varieties reduced and currently about 85 per cent of the Cotton area is under Bt cotton hybrids that require comparatively less seed

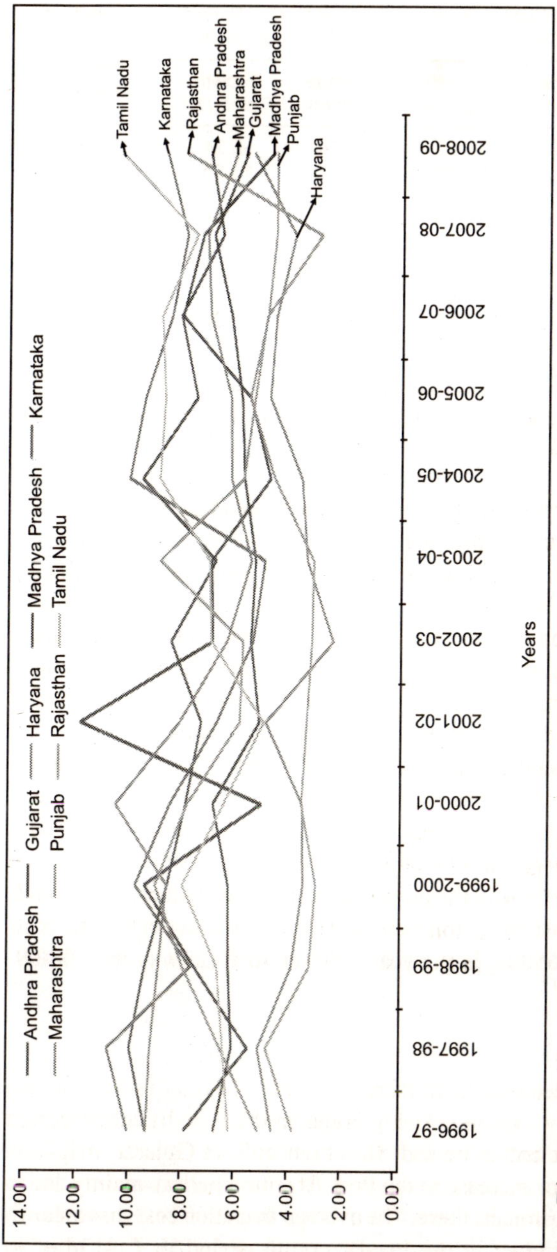

Source: Directorate of Economics and Statistics, Ministry of Agriculture and Cooperation, GoI.

Fig. 3.12: State-wise Proportion of Fertilizer Cost to Total Cost of Cotton (%)

Table 3.18: Seed Usage of Cotton in India

States	Pre-Bt Cotton Period (1996-97 to 2001-02)		Post-Bt Cotton Period (2002-03 to 2008-09)		2006-07 to 2008-09 Average (kg/hec)
	Average (kg/hec)	Growth Rates (%)	Average (kg/hec)	Growth Rates (%)	
Andhra Pradesh	4.10	6.83	1.94	–2.24	1.76
Gujarat	6.41	–9.19	3.81	–13.85	3.02
Haryana	12.10	–0.57	5.06	–31.75	3.91
Madhya Pradesh	6.31	–16.20	1.75	–11.75	1.38
Karnataka	7.53	2.62	4.94	–14.81	3.00
Maharashtra	3.89	5.14	3.46	–13.17	2.66
Punjab	15.15	–4.61	3.69	–23.67	2.51
Rajasthan	16.07	2.28	14.10	0.20	13.91
Tamil Nadu	11.03	–4.32	6.90	–12.87	6.13
India	9.23	–2.60	6.00	–13.25	4.24

Source: Directorate of Economics and Statistics, Ministry of Agriculture and Cooperation, GoI.

usage per hectare. Over the years, the Government data has shown a decline in the total seed usage per hectare in all the States. The trend growth rates of seed rates from the Pre to Post-Bt cotton period have also shown a significant decline. But during the last 3 years of available data it is observed that seed usage have reduced even further. The seed usage in the States of Rajasthan and Tamil Nadu are comparatively higher than the other States because here the proportion of Bt cotton and Non-Bt cotton are similar (CICR). In spite of using relatively less seed, farmers are realizing higher yields.

The proportion of seed cost to total cost of cotton has shown fluctuations in all the major cotton cultivating States within the range of 2 to 14 per cent. In recent years, the proportion of seed cost has shown a decline in the States of Madhya Pradesh, Punjab and Gujarat, whereas in the rest of the States it increased (Figure 3.13). Overall the proportions are showing increasing trends in most States in the Post-Bt cotton period. The all India average seed costs have increased from ₹ 650/kg in the year 2005-06 to ₹ 1239/kg in 2008-09.

Cotton Irrigation

From Table 3.19, it is seen that the trend growth rates in irrigation have shown a major decline in all the cotton growing States in the Post-Bt cotton period compared to the Pre-Bt cotton period. However, only in Gujarat, irrigation costs have shown a major increase in the Post-Bt cotton period, mainly due to several minor irrigation projects there. The average irrigation costs have shown an increase from ₹ 355/hec in the Pre-Bt cotton period to ₹ 813/hec in

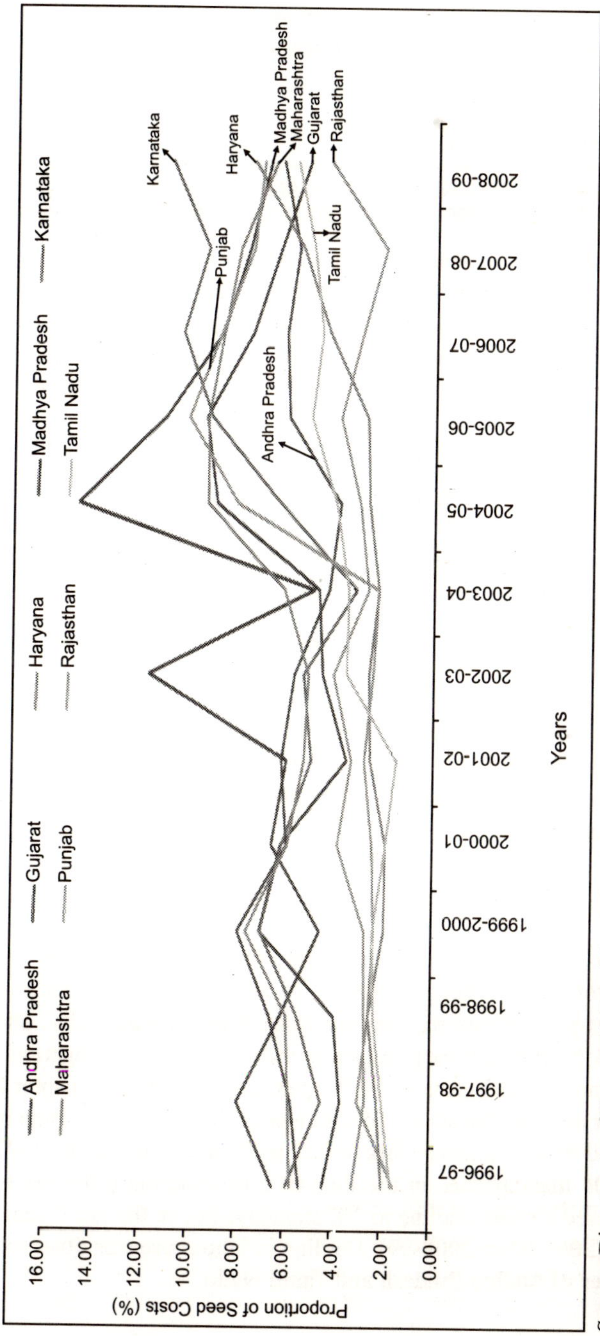

Source: Directorate of Economics and Statistics, Ministry of Agriculture and Cooperation, GoI.

Fig. 3.13: State-wise Proportion of Seed Cost to Total Cost of Cotton (%)

the Post-Bt cotton period, in response to increased diesel costs. However, during the last 3 years irrigation costs have reduced in most States, except Gujarat and Haryana, where it increased.

Table 3.19: Irrigation Cost of Cotton in India

States	Pre-Bt Cotton Period (1996-97 to 2001-02)		Pre-Bt Cotton Period (2002-03 to 2008-09)		2006-07 to 2008-09 Average (Rs/hec)
	Average (Rs/hec)	Growth Rates (%)	Average (Rs/hec)	Growth Rates (%)	
Andhra Pradesh	98	–15.50	180	–21.88	101
Gujarat	707	4.20	1652	12.05	1883
Haryana	826	21.39	2046	12.20	2058
Madhya Pradesh	225	–31.85	825	–15.74	534
Karnataka	67	90.20	171	–23.22	113
Maharashtra	195	36.62	442	–11.89	392
Punjab	492	15.62	649	–33.36	596
Rajasthan	480	12.51	585	–13.33	515
Tamil Nadu	770	32.33	827	–0.90	784
India	355	6.09	813	–0.25	775

Source: Directorate of Economics and Statistics, Ministry of Agriculture and Cooperation, GoI.

In terms of proportion of irrigation cost to total costs, it fluctuates from year to year in all the States, while in the States of Gujarat, Haryana, Maharashtra, Rajasthan and Andhra Pradesh, proportion of irrigation costs have also shown an increase since 2007-08 (Fig. 3.14).

Human Labour Use in Cotton

The proportion of human labour cost to total costs is the highest in the cultivation of cotton crop. It ranges between 25 and 50 per cent in various States. The highest proportions are seen for Tamil Nadu (around 40%) and Haryana (around 35%). Overall the proportions are showing increasing trends in the Post-Bt cotton period (Figure 3.15). Further, it will be seen in Chapter 8 that, human labour use after the advent of commercial Bt cotton cultivation in India, has increased from 96 mandays/hec in the Pre-Bt cotton period (1996-97 to 2001-02) to 104 mandays/hec in the Post-Bt cotton period (2002-03 to 2008-09) but showed a slight decline to 103 mandays/hec in the last 3 years of available data (2006-07 to 2008-09). Decline in labour use was observed mainly in the States of Andhra Pradesh and Tamil Nadu.

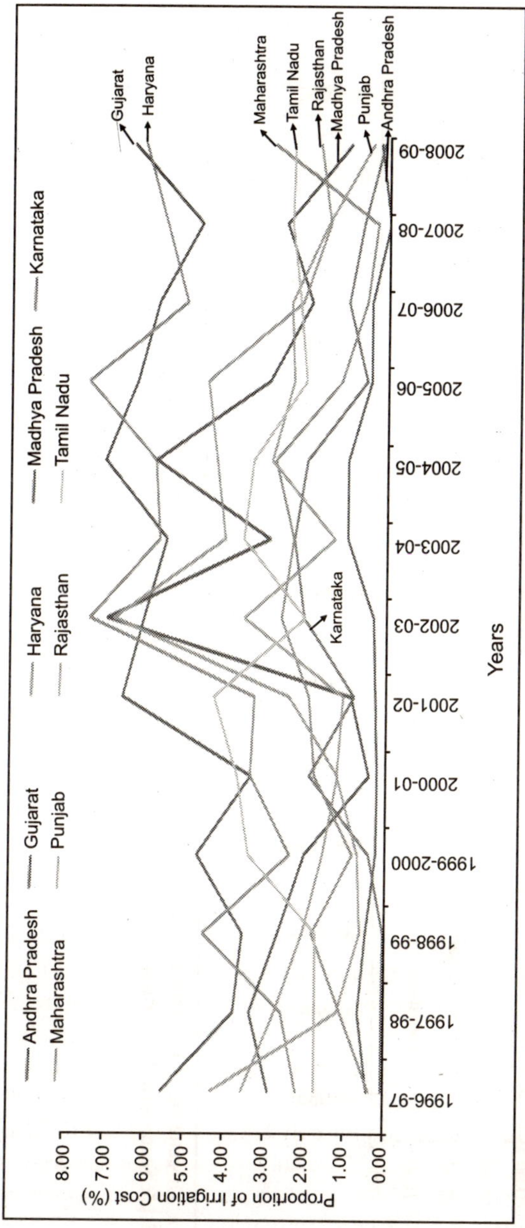

Source: Directorate of Economics and Statistics, Ministry of Agriculture and Cooperation, GoI.

Fig. 3.14: State-wise Proportion of Irrigation Cost to Total Cost of Cotton (%)

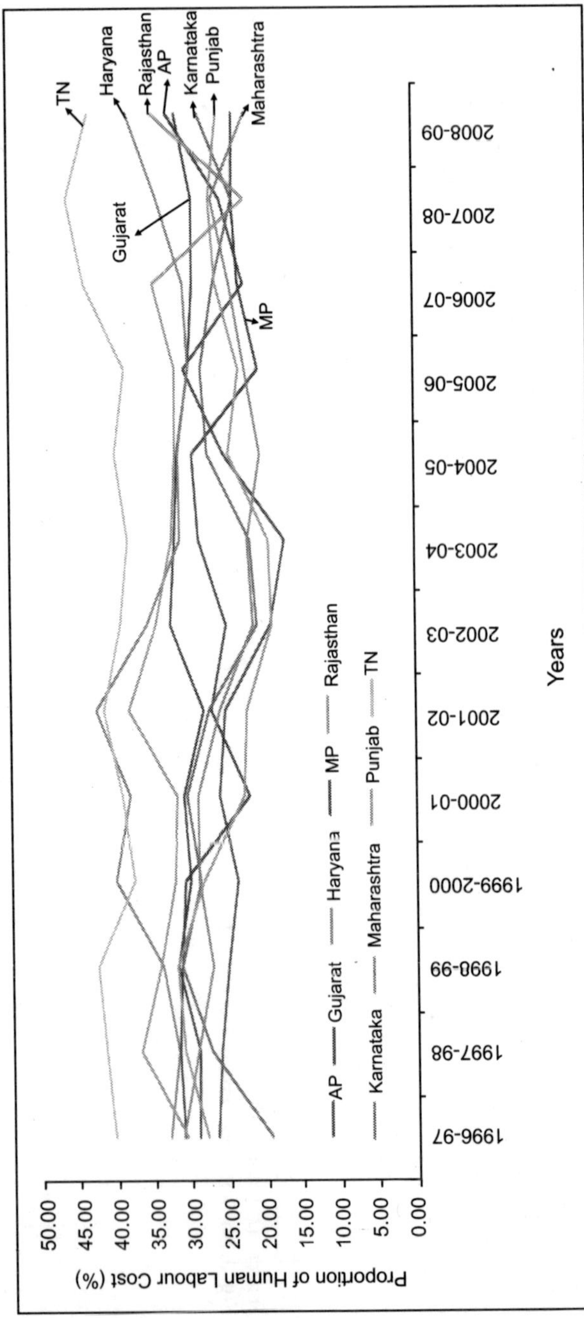

Source: Directorate of Economics and Statistics, Ministry of Agriculture and Cooperation, GoI.

Fig. 3.15: State-wise Proportion of Human Labour Cost to Total Cost of Cotton (%)

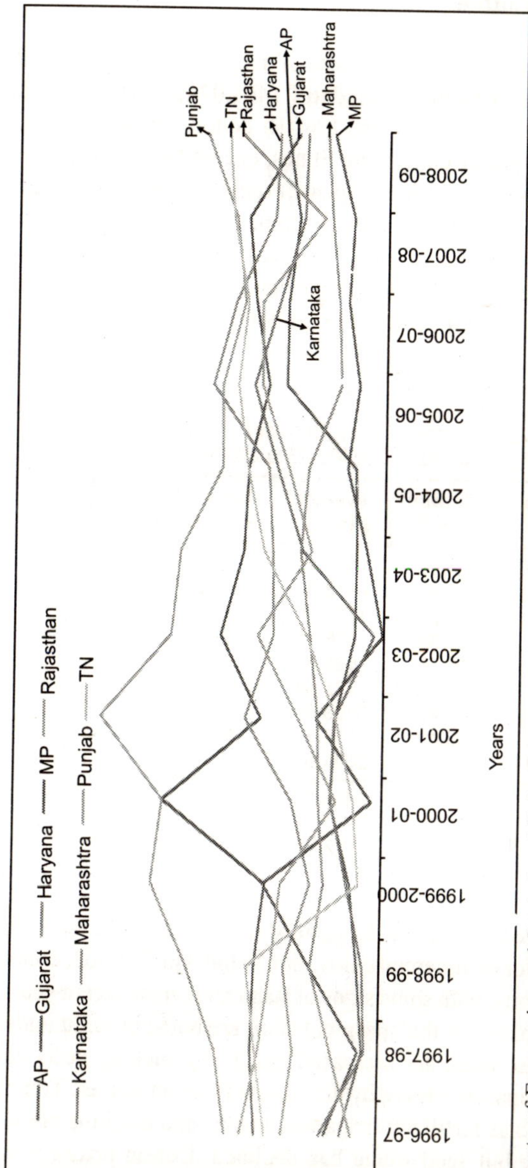

Source: Directorate of Economics and Statistics, Ministry of Agriculture and Cooperation, GoI.

Fig. 3.16: State-wise Proportion of Machine Labour Cost to Total Cost of Cotton (%)

Machine Labour Use in Cotton

Table 3.20 shows that average per hectare costs of machine labour increased from ₹ 732.06/hec in the Pre-Bt cotton period to ₹ 1408.07/hec in the Post-Bt cotton period. It grew at a high rate in the Post-Bt cotton period at the all India level and also in the major cultivating States, except Maharashtra and Haryana which showed a slight decline in growth rate in the Post-Bt cotton period. In the last 3 years of available data, machine labour costs increased for all the States. Further, Figure 3.16 shows that, costs of machine labour as a proportion of total costs show an increasing trend in the Post-Bt cotton period, except in Gujarat where it declined in 2008-09.

Table 3.20: Machine Labour Cost of Cotton in India (%)

States	Pre-Bt Cotton Period (1996-97 to 2001-02)		Post-Bt Cotton Period (2002-03 to 2008-09)		2006-07 to 2008-09 Average (Rs/hec)
	Average (Rs/hec)	Growth Rates (%)	Average (Rs/hec)	Growth Rates (%)	
Andhra Pradesh	373.59	12.90	1195.12	36.30	1870.68
Gujarat	962.38	6.44	1673.00	6.51	1849.59
Haryana	746.29	11.78	1782.00	–0.18	2134.91
Madhya Pradesh	264.30	10.36	410.70	59.56	610.83
Karnataka	199.17	16.16	625.31	37.65	821.51
Maharashtra	390.38	23.31	725.56	–0.21	733.44
Punjab	2082.99	13.47	3109.00	18.28	3317.99
Rajasthan	647.16	–0.49	1110.31	17.12	1454.04
Tamil Nadu	922.24	–19.67	2041.67	12.03	2412.20
India	732.06	7.07	1408.07	11.29	1689.47

Source: Directorate of Economics and Statistics, Ministry of Agriculture and Cooperation, GoI.

Thus it becomes clear from the foregoing discussion that with the introduction of Bt cotton for commercial cultivation in India in 2002-03, cotton yields increased significantly, with some signs of stagnation in the recent years. The reason for yield stagnation is that marginal lands are being brought under cotton cultivation and also there are increased attacks by sucking pests not sufficiently controlled by insecticides or by the current Bt technologies. Trends in input use in cotton such as fertilizer, irrigation, human and machine labour have shown an increase, but seed usage has declined. Cotton prices have increased but showed high fluctuations in recent years.

4

Economics of Cultivation of Bt Cotton

Results of Farm Level Survey

A field survey was undertaken in 2011-12 to carry out an in-depth analysis of the situation of Bt cotton growing farmers. In this chapter, data collected through field survey has been used extensively for detailed socio-economic analysis of Bt cotton.

Distribution of Area and Output of Bt Cotton by Farm Size Categories

It is seen from Table 4.1 that most Bt cotton growers surveyed across the country were small farmers (53.71%) followed by medium (36.76%) and then large farmers (9.52%). However exceptions existed in case of the districts of Bathinda in Punjab, Hissar in Haryana, Bhavnagar in Gujarat and Dhar and Khargone in Madhya Pradesh, where the shares of medium farmers were higher followed by small and then large farmers.

It is important to note that all farmers (100%) interviewed in the cotton growing areas cultivated Bt cotton. However, a small proportion of farmers (2.38%) from the districts of Sirsa in Haryana and Hanumangarh in Rajasthan, also cultivated Non-Bt (Desi) cotton. Most of them were cultivating it from 2003 onwards in the central and southern States whereas in the northern States they were cultivating it since 2005-06. Table 4.2 shows that total Bt-cotton area as a proportion of total cotton area is 98.90 per cent while the total Non-Bt (Desi) cotton area is only 1.10 per cent. Among all the major cotton cultivating States, Non-Bt (Desi) cotton is being cultivated only in the Sirsa district of Haryana and Hanumangarh district of Rajasthan with low shares of 3.76 per cent in the former and 9.24 per cent in the latter.

Cotton Productivity

Table 4.3 shows that the all India yields of Bt cotton (raw cotton) (23.17

Table 4.1: Number of Farmers in Different Land Size Categories

Region	*State*	*District*	*Small Farmers*	*Medium Farmers*	*Large Farmers*	*Total Farmers*
Northern Region	Punjab	Bathinda	20 (28.57)	45 (64.29)	5 (7.14)	70 (100)
		Fazilka	40 (57.14)	25 (35.71)	5 (7.14)	70 (100)
	Punjab Total		60 (42.86)	70 (50)	10 (7.14)	140 (100)
	Haryana	Hissar	24 (34.29)	34 (48.57)	12 (17.14)	70 (100)
		Sirsa	38 (54.29)	22 (31.43)	10 (14.29)	70 (100)
	Haryana Total		62 (44.29)	56 (40)	22 (15.71)	140 (100)
	Rajasthan	Hanumangarh	36 (51.43)	25 (35.71)	9 (12.86)	70 (100)
	Rajasthan Total		36 (51.43)	25 (35.71)	9 (12.86)	70 (100)
Central Region	Gujarat	Bhavnagar	29 (41.43)	37 (52.86)	4 (5.71)	70 (100)
		Surendranagar	48 (68.57)	20 (28.57)	2 (2.86)	70 (100)
	Gujarat Total		77 (55)	57 (40.71)	6 (4.29)	140 (100)
	Madhya Pradesh	Dhar	21 (30)	30 (42.86)	19 (27.14)	70 (100)
		Khargone	23 (32.86)	32 (45.71)	15 (21.43)	70 (100)
	Madhya Pradesh Total		44 (31.43)	62 (44.29)	34 (24.29)	140 (100)
	Maharashtra	Jalgaon	45 (64.29)	18 (25.71)	7 (10)	70 (100)
		Yavatmal	50 (71.43)	15 (21.43)	5 (7.14)	70 (100)
	Maharashtra Total		95 (67.86)	33 (23.57)	12 (8.57)	140 (100)
Southern Region	Andhra Pradesh	Adilabad	37 (52.86)	31 (44.29)	2 (2.86)	70 (100)
		Warangal	55 (78.57)	13 (18.57)	2 (2.86)	70 (100)
	Andhra Pradesh Total		92 (65.71)	44 (31.43)	4 (2.86)	140 (100)
	Karnataka	Dharwad	48 (68.57)	19 (27.14)	3 (4.29)	70 (100)
	Karnataka Total		48 (68.57)	19 (27.14)	3 (4.29)	70 (100)
	Tamil Nadu	Virudunagar	50 (71.43)	20 (28.57)	0 (0)	70 (100)
	Tamil Nadu Total		50 (71.43)	20 (28.57)	0 (0)	70 (100)
Grand Total			564 (53.71)	386 (36.76)	100 (9.52)	1050 (100)

Source: Primary Field Survey.

Note: Figures in parentheses are percentage to total.

Table 4.2: Bt Cotton and Non-Bt Cotton area as a Proportion of Total Cotton Area

Regions	*States*	*Districts*	*Farm Size Categories*	*Bt Cotton*	*Non-Bt (Desi) Cotton*
Northern Region	**Punjab**	**Bhatinda**	Small	100.00	0.00
			Medium	100.00	0.00
			Large	100.00	0.00
			Average	**100.00**	**0.00**
		Fazilka	Small	100.00	0.00
			Medium	100.00	0.00
			Large	100.00	0.00
			Average	**100.00**	**0.00**
		Punjab Average		**100.00**	**0.00**
	Haryana	**Hissar**	Small	100.00	0.00
			Medium	100.00	0.00
			Large	100.00	0.00
			Average	**100.00**	**0.00**
		Sirsa	Small	100.00	0.00
			Medium	96.08	3.92
			Large	82.99	17.01
			Average	**91.87**	**8.13**
		Haryana Average		**96.24**	**3.76**
	Rajasthan	**Hanumangarh**	Small	85.71	14.29
			Medium	89.12	10.88
			Large	100.00	0.00
			Average	**90.76**	**9.24**
		Rajasthan Average		**90.76**	**9.24**
Central Region	**Gujarat**	**Bhavnagar**	Small	100.00	0.00
			Medium	100.00	0.00
			Large	100.00	0.00
			Average	**100.00**	**0.00**
		Surendranagar	Small	100.00	0.00
			Medium	100.00	0.00
			Large	100.00	0.00
			Average	**100.00**	**0.00**
		Gujarat Average		**100.00**	**0.00**
	Madhya Pradesh	**Dhar**	Small	100.00	0.00
			Medium	100.00	0.00
			Large	100.00	0.00
			Average	**100.00**	**0.00**
		Khargone	Small	100.00	0.00
			Medium	100.00	0.00
			Large	100.00	0.00
			Average	**100.00**	**0.00**
		Madhya Pradesh Average		**100.00**	**0.00**
	Maharashtra	**Jalgaon**	Small	100.00	0.00
			Medium	100.00	0.00
			Large	100.00	0.00
			Average	**100.00**	**0.00**
		Yavatmal	Small	100.00	0.00
			Medium	100.00	0.00
			Large	100.00	0.00
			Average	**100.00**	**0.00**
		Maharashtra Average		**100.00**	**0.00**

(*Contd.*)

Table 4.2 (*Contd.*)

Regions	*States*	*Districts*	*Farm Size Categories*	*Bt Cotton*	*Non-Bt (Desi) Cotton*
Southern Region	**Andhra Pradesh**	**Adilabad**	Small	100.00	0.00
			Medium	100.00	0.00
			Large	100.00	0.00
			Average	**100.00**	**0.00**
		Warangal	Small	100.00	0.00
			Medium	100.00	0.00
			Large	100.00	0.00
			Average	**100.00**	**0.00**
		Andhra Pradesh Average		**100.00**	**0.00**
	Karnataka	**Dharwad**	Small	100.00	0.00
			Medium	100.00	0.00
			Large	100.00	0.00
			Average	**100.00**	**0.00**
		Karnataka Average		**100.00**	**0.00**
	Tamil Nadu	**Virudunagar**	Small	100.00	0.00
			Medium	100.00	0.00
			Large		
			Average	**100.00**	**0.00**
		Tamil Nadu Average		**100.00**	**0.00**
ALL INDIA			Small	98.98	1.02
			Medium	98.93	1.07
			Large	98.81	1.19
			Average	**98.90**	**1.10**

Source: Primary Field Survey.

qtl/hec) are slightly higher than those of Non-Bt (Desi) cotton (20.11 qtl/ hec) for the agricultural year 2010-11. The survey districts that show yields greater than the national average are Virudunagar in Tamil Nadu (37.25 qtl/hec) followed by Surendranagar in Gujarat (33.42 qtl/hec), Warangal in Andhra Pradesh (33.15 qtl/hec) and Hanumangarh in Rajasthan (25.66 qtl/hec). The yields of Bt cotton are neutral to farm size.

As regards cotton prices it is seen in chapter 3, that cotton prices, both in terms of minimum support prices as well as farm harvest prices have shown an upward trend in the Post-Bt cotton period along with high fluctuations indicating instability in prices. The Minimum Support Price (MSP) for long staple length cotton in the country in 2010-11 was ₹ 3000/qtl. The field survey shows that farmers in all the States sold cotton above the MSP except in Tamil Nadu (Table 4.4).

Table 4.3: Cotton Productivity (Raw Cotton) (qtl/hec)

Regions	*States*	*Districts*	*Farm Size Categories*	*Bt Cotton*	*Non-Bt (Desi) Cotton*
Northern Region	**Punjab**	**Bhatinda**	Small	19.46	
			Medium	19.07	
			Large	18.28	
			District Average	**19.12**	
		Fazilka	Small	20.11	
			Medium	20.95	
			Large	19.76	
			District Average	20.38	
		Punjab Average		**19.76**	
	Haryana	**Hissar**	Small	20.60	
			Medium	21.02	
			Large	21.51	
			District Average	**20.97**	
		Sirsa	Small	19.56	
			Medium	21.74	19.76
			Large	21.27	19.14
			District Average	**20.50**	**19.46**
		Haryana Average		**20.72**	**19.46**
	Rajasthan	**Hanumangarh**	Small	26.08	20.58
			Medium	26.60	21.00
			Large	21.41	
			District Average	**25.66**	**20.75**
		Rajasthan Average		**25.66**	**20.75**
Central Region	**Gujarat**	**Bhavnagar**	Small	27.76	
			Medium	28.38	
			Large	24.13	
			District Average	**27.89**	
		Surendranagar	Small	33.12	
			Medium	34.21	
			Large	32.48	
			District Average	**33.42**	
		Gujarat Average		**30.65**	
	Madhya Pradesh	**Dhar**	Small	16.57	
			Medium	15.26	
			Large	13.78	
			District Average	**15.26**	

(Contd.)

Table 4.3 (*Contd.*)

Regions	*States*	*Districts*	*Farm Size Categories*	*Bt Cotton*	*Non-Bt (Desi) Cotton*
		Khargone	Small	18.77	
			Medium	19.32	
			Large	17.73	
			District Average	**18.80**	
		Madhya Pradesh Average		**17.02**	
	Maharashtra	**Jalgaon**	Small	18.06	
			Medium	15.04	
			Large	11.83	
			District Average	**16.65**	
		Yavatmal	Small	18.85	
			Medium	20.16	
			Large	24.43	
			District Average	**19.51**	
		Maharashtra Average		**18.08**	
Southern Region	**Andhra Pradesh**	**Adilabad**	Small	18.40	
			Medium	19.09	
			Large	18.53	
			District Average	**18.70**	
		Warangal	Small	32.16	
			Medium	37.35	
			Large	33.35	
			District Average	**33.15**	
		Andhra Pradesh Average		**25.94**	
	Karnataka	**Dharwad**	Small	18.99	
			Medium	21.71	
			Large	27.99	
			District Average	**20.11**	
		Karnataka Average		**20.11**	
	Tamil Nadu	**Virudunagar**	Small	35.79	
			Medium	40.88	
			Large	0.00	
			District Average	**37.25**	
		Tamil Nadu Average		**37.25**	
ALL INDIA			Small	22.95	10.30
			Medium	24.06	20.38
			Large	20.43	9.58
			All India Average	**23.17**	**20.11**

Source: Primary Field Survey.

Cotton Prices

Table 4.4: Average Selling Price of Bt Cotton Hybrids in 2010-11 (₹/qtl)

Regions	*States*	*Districts*	*Farm Size Categories*	*Selling Price*
Northern Region	**Punjab**	**Bhatinda**	Small	5118.50
			Medium	5231.33
			Large	5080.00
			District Average	**5188.29**
		Fazilka	Small	5427.00
			Medium	5694.00
			Large	5880.00
			District Average	**5554.71**
		Punjab Average		**5371.50**
	Haryana	**Hissar**	Small	5337.69
			Medium	5442.79
			Large	5647.92
			District Average	**5441.92**
		Sirsa	Small	4514.04
			Medium	4784.47
			Large	4833.33
			District Average	**4644.64**
		Haryana Average		**5043.28**
	Rajasthan	**Hanumangarh**	Small	5094.28
			Medium	5112.07
			Large	5281.11
			District Average	**5124.65**
		Rajasthan Average		**5124.65**
Central Region	**Gujarat**	**Bhavnagar**	Small	4045.69
			Medium	4195.27
			Large	3850.00
			District Average	**4113.57**
		Surendranagar	Small	4163.02
			Medium	4112.92
			Large	4600.00
			District Average	**4161.19**
		Gujarat Average		**4137.38**
	Madhya Pradesh	**Dhar**	Small	3857.14
			Medium	4153.89
			Large	4350.44
			District Average	**4118.21**
		Khargone	Small	4291.30
			Medium	4343.75
			Large	4408.89
			District Average	**4340.48**
		Madhya Pradesh Average		**4229.35**

(Contd.)

Table 4.4 (*Contd.*)

Regions	*States*	*Districts*	*Farm Size Categories*	*Selling Price*
	Maharashtra	**Jalgaon**	Small	4100.04
			Medium	4038.67
			Large	4165.03
			District Average	**4090.76**
		Yavatmal	Small	4059.90
			Medium	3895.66
			Large	3826.51
			District Average	**4008.03**
		Maharashtra Average		**4049.40**
Southern Region	**Andhra Pradesh**	**Adilabad**	Small	3821.62
			Medium	3809.01
			Large	3900.00
			District Average	**3818.27**
		Warangal	Small	4187.09
			Medium	4226.92
			Large	4000.00
			District Average	**4189.14**
		Andhra Pradesh Average		**4003.71**
	Karnataka	**Dharwad**	Small	4550.00
			Medium	4878.95
			Large	6000.00
			District Average	**4701.43**
		Karnataka Average		**4701.43**
	Tamil Nadu	**Virudunagar**	Small	2172.67
			Medium	2150.00
			Large	
			District Average	**2166.19**
		Tamil Nadu Average		**2166.19**
ALL INDIA			Small	**4229.70**
			Medium	**4499.57**
			Large	**4739.18**
			All India Average	**4377.43**

Source: Primary Field Survey.

Irrigated Area under Cotton

From the primary field survey it was seen that Bt cotton was mostly cultivated under unirrigated or rainfed conditions in India (55.59%). The rest 44.41 per cent cotton area was irrigated (Table 4.5). Non-Bt (Desi) cotton was cultivated under irrigated conditions in the Northern States. Both Bt cotton and Non-Bt (Desi) cotton was cultivated under irrigated conditions in the Northern States of Punjab, Haryana and Rajasthan. In the rest of the Central and Southern regions covering the States of Gujarat, Madhya Pradesh, Maharashtra, Andhra

Pradesh, Karnataka and Tamil Nadu, the share of unirrigated Cotton area was found to be higher. Amongst these States the area share of unirrigated Cotton was highest in Madhya Pradesh (98.08%) followed closely by Andhra Pradesh (92.61%), Tamil Nadu (86.33%), Maharashtra (79.15%) and lastly Gujarat (60.54%). In Gujarat, the area share under irrigated Cotton was comparatively greater than that of the other central and southern states because of several micro-irrigation schemes there (Table 4.5). Further, it was also seen that small farmers have a relatively higher proportion of area under unirrigated cotton compared to medium and large farmers but put in more area under irrigated Cotton.

Table 4.5: Total Irrigated and Unirrigated Area under Cotton (%)

Region	*State*	*District*	*Farm Size Categories*	*Bt Cotton*		*Non-Bt (Desi) Cotton*	
				Irrigated Area	*Unirrigated Area*	*Irrigated Area*	*Unirrigated Area*
Northern Region	Punjab	Bhatinda	Small	100.00			
			Medium	100.00			
			Large	100.00			
			Average	100.00			
		Fazilka	Small	100.00			
			Medium	100.00			
			Large	100.00			
			Average	100.00			
		Punjab Average		100.00			
	Haryana	Hissar	Small	100.00			
			Medium	100.00			
			Large	100.00			
			Average	100.00			
		Sirsa	Small	100.00			
			Medium	100.00		100.00	
			Large	100.00		100.00	
			Average	100.00		100.00	
		Haryana Average		100.00		100.00	
	Rajasthan	Hanumangarh	Small	100.00		100.00	
			Medium	100.00		100.00	
			Large	100.00			
			Average	100.00		100.00	
		Rajasthan Average		100.00		100.00	
Central Region	Gujarat	Bhavnagar	Small	38.54	61.46		
			Medium	30.58	69.42		
			Large	40.87	59.13		
			Average	36.66	63.34		
		Surendranagar	Small	42.82	57.18		
			Medium	40.51	59.49		
			Large	43.46	56.54		
			Average	42.26	57.74		
		Gujarat Average		39.46	60.54		

(Contd.)

Table 4.5 (*Contd.*)

Region	*State*	*District*	*Farm Size Categories*	*Bt Cotton*		*Non-Bt (Desi) Cotton*	
				Irrigated Area	*Unirrigated Area*	*Irrigated Area*	*Unirrigated Area*
	Madhya Pradesh	Dhar	Small	—	100.00		
			Medium	5.02	94.98		
			Large	—	100.00		
			Average	1.98	98.02		
		Khargone	Small	2.56	97.44		
			Medium	0.44	99.56		
			Large	2.61	97.39		
			Average	1.87	98.13		
		Madhya Pradesh Average		1.93	98.08		
	Maharashtra	Jalgaon	Small	22.73	77.27		
			Medium	20.99	79.01		
			Large	25.45	74.55		
			Average	23.06	76.94		
		Yavatmal	Small	10.12	89.88		
			Medium	22.47	77.53		
			Large	23.33	76.67		
			Average	18.64	81.36		
		Maharashtra Average		20.85	79.15		
Southern Region	Andhra Pradesh	Adilabad	Small	3.59	96.41		
			Medium	1.89	98.11		
			Large	—	100.00		
			Average	2.07	97.93		
		Warangal	Small	9.26	90.74		
			Medium	3.31	96.69		
			Large	—	100.00		
			Average	5.00	95.00		
		Andhra Pradesh Average		7.39	92.61		
	Karnataka	Dharwad	Small	16.96	83.04		
			Medium	27.78	72.22		
			Large	18.75	81.25		
			Average	21.00	79.00		
		Karnataka Average		21.00	79.00		
	Tamil Nadu	Virudunagar	Small	13.02	86.98		
			Medium	14.75	85.25		
			Large	—	—		
			Average	13.67	86.33		
		Tamil Nadu Average		13.67	86.33		
ALL INDIA			Small	43.97	56.03	100.00	
			Medium	44.52	55.48	100.00	
			Large	43.63	56.37	100.00	
			Average	44.41	55.59	100.00	

Source: Primary Field Survey.

Table 4.6 shows the average seed packets used (400-450 grams/packet) for both Bt and Non-Bt cotton per hectare in the surveyed regions. It is seen that the average Bt cotton seed usage is 4 packets/hec. Bt cotton seed usage is less (3 packets/hec) than Non-Bt (Desi) cotton (5 packets/hec) seed usage in the Sirsa district of Haryana. The differences between small, medium and large farmers on seed usage are negligible.

Seed Usage

Table 4.6: Average Seed Packets used Per Hectare (1 Packet = 450 gams)

Regions	*States*	*Districts*	*Farm Size Categories*	*Bt Cotton*	*Non-Bt (Desi) Cotton*
Northern Region	**Punjab**	**Bhatinda**	Small	6	0
			Medium	6	0
			Large	5	0
			District Average	**6**	0
		Fazilka	Small	5	0
			Medium	5	0
			Large	5	0
			District Average	**5**	0
		Punjab Average		**5**	**0**
	Haryana	**Hissar**	Small	5	0
			Medium	5	0
			Large	5	0
			District Average	**5**	0
		Sirsa	Small	3	0
			Medium	3	4
			Large	3	5
			District Average	**3**	**5**
		Haryana Average		**4**	**5**
	Rajasthan	**Hanumangarh**	Small	5	5
			Medium	5	5
			Large	5	0
			District Average	**5**	**5**
		Rajasthan Average		**5**	**5**
Central Region	**Gujarat**	**Bhavnagar**	Small	5	0
			Medium	5	0
			Large	5	0
			District Average	**5**	0
		Surendranagar	Small	6	0
			Medium	6	0
			Large	5	0
			District Average	**6**	0
		Gujarat Average		**6**	**0**
	Madhya Pradesh	**Dhar**	Small	3	0
			Medium	4	0
			Large	4	0
			District Average	**4**	0

(Contd.)

Table 4.6 (*Contd.*)

Regions	*States*	*Districts*	*Farm Size Categories*	*Bt Cotton*	*Non-Bt (Desi) Cotton*
		Khargone	Small	5	0
			Medium	5	0
			Large	5	0
			District Average	**5**	0
		Madhya Pradesh Average		**4**	0
	Maharashtra	**Jalgaon**	Small	3	0
			Medium	4	0
			Large	5	0
			District Average	**3**	0
		Yavatmal	Small	2	0
			Medium	3	0
			Large	3	0
			District Average	**3**	0
		Maharashtra Average		**3**	0
Southern Region	**Andhra Pradesh**	**Adilabad**	Small	3	0
			Medium	4	0
			Large	2	0
			District Average	3	0
		Warangal	Small	4	0
			Medium	4	0
			Large	3	0
			District Average	4	0
		Andhra Pradesh Average		**4**	**0**
	Karnataka	**Dharwad**	Small	3	0
			Medium	4	0
			Large	3	0
			District Average	3	0
		Karnataka Average		**3**	**0**
	Tamil Nadu	**Virudunagar**	Small	7	0
			Medium	7	0
			Large	0	0
			District Average	7	0
		Tamil Nadu Average		**7**	**0**
ALL INDIA			Small	4	5
			Medium	5	5
			Large	4	5
			All India Average	**4**	**5**

Source: Primary Field Survey.

Regarding seeds, it needs to be mentioned that there are over a 1000 Bt hybrid seeds that are being used by farmers in the study region. All these seeds are being made and marketed by private sector companies that pay royalty to Monsanto Seed Company, which has a patent for the Bt gene.

Recently in the year 2009, the Central Institute of Cotton Research (CICR), a public sector institute, in collaboration with the University of Agricultural Sciences (UAS), Dharwad, developed a Bt cotton variety called 'Bikaneri Narma'. This was the only public sector variety of Bt cotton in India. They also indigenously developed a Bt cotton hybrid called NHH-44 Bt. However, farmers in the survey region have not used it, mainly because they do not have information about it.

Table 4.7 shows the proportion of farmers using Bt cotton seeds from different seed companies in the surveyed regions. It is found that a high proportion of farmers (25.14%) used seeds of Nuziveedu Seeds Pvt. Ltd. of Andhra Pradesh, followed by Shriram Bioseeds Genetics of Andhra Pradesh (20.57%), Rasi Seeds Pvt. Ltd. of Tamil Nadu (19.24%), Ankur Seeds Pvt. Ltd. of Maharashtra (17.24%), Bayer Biosciences Pvt. Ltd. of Andhra Pradesh (14.95%), Mahyco Ltd. (13.62%) and Monsanto Holdings Pvt. Ltd. of Maharashtra (6.29%).

In the State of Punjab the share of Shriram Bioseeds Genetics was the highest (above 70%). In Haryana the share of Rasi Seeds Pvt. Ltd. was the highest (above 35%). In the State of Rajasthan the share of Shriram Bioseeds Genetics was the highest (78.57%) followed by Rasi Seeds Pvt. Ltd. (54.29%). In Gujarat the share of Ajeet Seeds Pvt. Ltd. was the highest (above 20%) followed by Nuziveedu Seeds Pvt. Ltd. (above 15%). In the State of Madhya Pradesh the share of Ajeet Seeds Pvt. Ltd. was the highest (above 60%) followed by Ankur Seeds Pvt. Ltd. (above 35%). In the State of Maharashtra the share of Nuziveedu Seeds Pvt. Ltd. was the highest (above 60%) followed by Ankur Seeds Pvt. Ltd. (around 50%). In Karnataka the share of Mahyco Maharashtra Hybrid Seeds Co. Ltd. was the highest (30%) followed by Nuziveedu Seeds Pvt . Ltd. (22%). In the State of Andhra Pradesh the share of Mahyco Maharashtra Hybrid Seeds Co. Ltd. was the highest in Warangal district (57.14%), while in Adilabad district the share of Nuziveedu Seeds Pvt. Ltd. was the highest (41.43%). In Tamil Nadu the share of Nuziveedu Seeds Pvt. Ltd. was the highest (above 54.29%) followed by Rasi Seeds Pvt. Ltd. (38.57%).

Bt Cotton—Cost of Cultivation

To understand the economics of Bt cotton production, an analysis of cost of cultivation was undertaken. Data collected through field survey was used extensively for the detailed analysis. The present study follows the methodology adopted by the Directorate of Economics and Statistics, Ministry of Agriculture, Government of India in its annual report 'Comprehensive Scheme for Studying the Cost of Cultivation of Principle Crops in India'. Herein, total costs are the total working capital which includes cost of seed, fertiliser, micronutrients,

Table 4.7: Proportion of Farmers using Seeds from Different Companies (%)

Seed Companies	Punjab		Haryana		Rajasthan	Gujarat		Madhya Pradesh		Maharashtra		Andhra Pradesh		Karnataka	Tamil Nadu	All India
	Bathinda	Fazilka	Hisar	Sirsa	Hanuman-garh	Surendra-nagar	Bhav nagar	Dhar	Khargone	Yavatmal	Jalgaon	Warangal	Adilabad	Dharwad	Virudu-nagar	
Krishidhan Seeds Pvt. Ltd. Maharashtra	12.86	11.43	—	—	—	—	—	—	2.86	27.14	22.86	—	5.71	—	—	5.52
Ankur Seeds Pvt. Ltd. Maharashtra	14.29	12.86	34.29	4.29	—	2.86	1.43	35.71	38.57	64.29	48.57	—	—	1.43	—	17.24
Rasi Seeds Pvt. Ltd., Tamil Nadu	5.71	4.29	34.29	48.57	54.29	10.00	15.71		1.43	18.57	37.14		18.57	1.43	38.57	1924
J.K. Agri Genetics Ltd., A.P.	57.14	61.43	—	—	—	—	—	—	2.86	—	11.43	—	—	—	—	8.86
Shriram Bioseed Genetics, A.P.	78.57	71.43	15.71	47.14	78.57	—	—	—	—	10.00	7.14	—	—	—	—	20.57
Mahyco, Maharashtra Hybrid Seeds Co. Ltd., Maharashtra	47.14	45.71	—	2.86	2.86	7.14	1.43	—	—	—	5.71	57.14	4.29	30.00	—	13.62
Nuziveedu Seeds Pvt. Ltd., AP	21.43	25.71	—	2.86	—	17.14	10.00	1.43	—	77.14	65.71	37.14	41.43	22.86	54.29	25.14
Tulasi Seeds Pvt. Ltd. AP	1.43	1.43	—	—	4.29	2.86	1.43	—	—	17.14	10.00	7.14	30.00	4.29	—	5.33
Kaveri seeds Co. Ltd. AP	10.00	11.43	10.00	—	—	—	—	—	—	—	—	7.14	—	14.29	7.14	4.00
Vibha Agrotech Ltd., AP	15.71	18.57	8.57	7.14	—	—	1.43	—	—	18.57	12.86	—	—	—	—	5.52
Monsanto Holdings Pvt. Ltd., Maharashtra	12.86	14.29	—	1.43	—	—	—	1.43	—	38.57	20.00	2.86	1.43	1.43	—	6.29
Namdhari Seeds Pvt. Ltd. Karnataka	1.43	2.86	—	—	—	—	—	—	—	—	—	—	—	—	—	0.29
Navbharat Seeds Pvt. Ltd., Gujarat	—	—	1.43	—	—	10.00	10.00	—	—	—	—	—	—	—	—	1.43
Amar Bio-Tech Ltd., AP	—	—	—	32.86	11.43	—	—	—	—	—	—	—	—	—	—	2.95
Bayer Biosciences Pvt. Ltd., AP	—	—	—	1.43	—	—	—	—	—	27.14	7.14	—	1.43	—	—	2.48
Ajeet Seeds Ltd, Maharashtra	—	—	—	—	—	24.29	15.71	65.71	77.14	7.14	31.43	2.86	—	—	—	14.95
Sri Sathya Agri Biotech Pvt. Ltd. AP	—	—	—	—	—	—	—	—	—	5.71	4.29	—	11.73	—	—	1.43
Global Transgenes Ltd., (Nath), Aurangabad	—	—	—	—	—	—	—	—	—	—	2.86	—	—	—	—	0.19
Vikram Seeds Pvt.. Gujarat	—	—	—	—	—	7.14	4.29	—	—	—	1.43	—	—	—	—	0.86
Seedworks International Pvt. Ltd., AP	—	—	—	—	—	—	—	—	—	—	7.14	—	—	—	—	0.48
Prabhat Agri Biotech Ltd., Hyderabad	—	—	—	—	—	—	—	—	—	—	1.43	—	—	—	—	0.19
Pravardhan Seeds Pvt. Ltd., AP	—	—	—	—	—	—	—	—	—	—	—	1.43	—	—	—	0.10

Source: Primary Field Survey.

growth regulators, farmyard manure, pesticide, irrigation, farm mechanisation and human labour costs (includes imputed value of family labour).

From Table 4.8 it is seen that, the total working capital costs of cultivating Bt cotton in India is ₹ 29496.78/hec. The highest cost was seen in case of Gujarat (₹ 35184.30/hec) followed by Andhra Pradesh (₹ 34135.19/hec), Haryana (₹ 33303.83/hec), Punjab (₹ 32177.017/hec), Maharashtra (₹ 28675.39/hec) and Madhya Pradesh (₹ 24748.77/hec). Relatively lower costs were seen for Karnataka (₹ 24320.42/hec) and Rajasthan (₹ 22034.99/hec). Gujarat reported higher costs because of higher costs for usage of fertilizer and farm yard manure, especially in the Bhavnagar district compared to other districts and states.

Among individual farm input costs, average seed cost in the country was ₹ 2834.25/hec. Seed costs were highest for Punjab (₹ 4077.35/hec) and lowest for Madhya Pradesh (₹ 946.27/hec) and Andhra Pradesh (₹ 965.43/hec). The average fertilizer cost in the country was ₹ 2337.28/hec. In case of fertilizers highest cost was reported in Tamil Nadu (₹ 4765.15/hec) and the lowest was seen in Madhya Pradesh (₹ 2768.57/hec). The all India growth regulator cost was ₹ 89/hec, with the highest cost Maharashtra (₹ 427.97/hec) especially Yavatmal (₹ 628.20/hec) and the lowest in Haryana (₹ 19.22/hec) and Madhya Pradesh (₹ 9.18/hec). The average cost of farmyard manure was ₹ 1226.40/hec, with the highest in Maharashtra (₹ 3598.52/hec) and lowest in Tamil Nadu (₹ 33.75/hec). The average micronutrient cost of India was ₹ 287.89/hec, with the highest in Maharashtra (₹ 741.12/hec) and lowest in Madhya Pradesh (₹ 5.09/hec). The average pesticide cost in India was ₹ 2627.30/hec with the highest in Punjab (₹ 3996.40/hec) and the lowest in Tamil Nadu (₹ 1899.53/hec). The average irrigation cost in the country was ₹ 1079.56/hec. In case of irrigation, highest cost was reported in Gujarat (₹ 3010.70/hec) and the lowest was seen in Karnataka (₹ 299.74/hec) and Punjab (₹ 300.756/hec). Compared to other input costs the costs of human labour were very high (₹ 15540.88/hec). They were found to be the highest in the Sirsa district of Haryana (₹ 23348.82/hec) and Andhra Pradesh (₹ 21553.79/hec). The lowest human labour cost was seen in Rajasthan (11223.70/hec).

Further it was observed that the per hectare cost of cultivation declined across farm size categories, suggesting economies of scale in input costs for large farmers. Cost of cultivation of Bt cotton has not been compared with Non-Bt (Desi) cotton because a very small proportion of farmers were cultivating the latter (2.38%).

The average value of output or gross returns from Bt cotton at the all India level was ₹ 94804.60/hec. The highest value of output was seen in the Hanumangarh district of Rajasthan (₹ 132981.41/hec). This was followed by Gujarat (₹ 122198.97/hec) wherein the contribution of Surendranagar was ₹ 138412.19/hec. The gross returns from Warangal district of Andhra Pradesh

Table 4.8: Bt Cotton—Cost of Cultivation (₹/hec)

Regions	States	Districts	Farm Size Categories	Seed Cost (Rs/hec)	Fertilizer Cost (Rs/hec)	Growth Regulators Cost (Rs/hec)	FYM Cost (Rs/hec)	Micro-nutrient Cost (Rs/hec)	Pesticide Cost (Rs/hec)	Irrigation Charges (Rs/hec)	Mechanisation Cost (Rs/hec)	Human Labour Cost (Rs/hec)	Total cost (Rs/hec)	Gross Returns (Rs/hec)	Net Returns (Rs/hec)
Northern Region	Punjab	Bhatinda	Small	3710.23	3325.90	42.39	95.68	514.46	3469.68	636.29	5401.95	19554.40	36750.97	100834.59	64083.61
			Medium	4114.48	3586.84	13.39	0.00	554.67	3730.91	226.04	5047.31	17470.84	34744.48	102801.45	68056.98
			Large	2722.80	3700.97	0.00	0.00	340.86	4314.44	210.72	4051.71	16611.46	31952.97	91496.70	59543.74
			District Average	3822.56	3576.13	14.46	11.27	512.40	3802.56	271.68	4914.33	17565.47	34490.87	100585.31	66094.44
		Fazilka	Small	4240.53	2712.12	111.35	623.38	704.30	3826.44	611.54	5223.46	15999.99	34053.11	111533.67	77480.56
			Medium	4331.45	2744.91	295.40	219.02	807.54	4288.79	254.22	4078.96	11886.70	28906.99	121978.14	93071.15
			Large	4381.08	3082.43	267.03	287.05	710.29	4265.26	247.00	3807.54	11581.03	28628.70	115102.00	86473.30
			District Average	4324.47	2822.73	248.88	322.65	761.00	4183.93	328.87	4255.66	12690.09	29938.28	118014.70	88076.42
		Punjab Average		4077.65	3193.21	133.60	169.53	638.75	3996.40	300.75	4579.56	15087.55	32177.01	109443.84	77266.83
	Haryana	Hissar	Small	3081.25	3352.97	0.00	0.00	58.75	2781.75	2729.55	2677.58	1921726	33899.12	100532.17	66633.05
			Medium	3169.72	3439.26	0.00	155.02	141.69	3358.61	2237.57	3100.96	15034.06	30636.89	115575.02	84938.13
			Large	3477.55	3252.85	0.00	295.43	31.63	2787.65	1581.55	3317.06	13817.73	28561.45	120553.24	91991.79
			District Average	3269.66	3351.29	0.00	178.10	83.47	3027.80	2084.14	3100.21	15391.65	30486.31	114519.40	84033.09
		Sirsa	Small	2996.58	1940.68	0.00	0.00	252.39	2226.29	2499.42	2626.66	23616.54	36158.57	91710.75	55552.18
			Medium	2773.43	2703.92	75.49	0.00	415.72	2705.47	2381.18	2441.89	23511.84	37008.95	104694.42	67685.47
			Large	2960.01	3456.62	46.02	414.22	530.36	3036.74	1410.93	2462.73	22977.79	37295.43	107053.79	69758.36
			District Average	2903.68	2759.95	43.56	149.36	410.97	2689.70	2064.69	2501.55	23348.82	36872.28	101381.24	65008.97
		Haryana Average		3108.19	3090.39	19.22	165.42	227.96	2878.63	2075.56	2836.08	18902.39	33303.83	108943.38	75639.54
	Rajasthan	Hanumangarh	Small	1866.39	3162.90	0.00	0.00	442.54	1800.71	629.84	2998.68	13089.74	23990.81	131991.20	108000.39
			Medium	1767.95	3316.47	0.00	0.00	493.16	2275.41	556.42	2767.84	10813.55	21990.81	137583.31	115692.50
			Large	1909.77	2286.45	182.96	0.00	698.19	2025.77	453.65	2375.00	10461.26	20393.04	123587.09	103194.05
			District Average	1824.24	3030.14	44.91	0.00	532.44	2110.57	547.21	2721.78	11223.70	22034.99	132981.41	110946.42
		Rajasthan Average		1824.24	3030.14	44.91	0.00	532.44	2110.57	547.21	2721.78	11223.70	22034.99	132981.41	110946.42

(Contd.)

Table 4.8 (*Contd.*)

Regions	States	Districts	Farm Size Categories	Seed Cost Rs/hec)	Fertilizer Cost (Rs/hec)	Growth Regulators Cost (Rs/hec)	FYM Cost (Rs/hec)	Micro-nutrient Cost (Rs/hec)	Pesticide Cost (Rs/hec)	Irrigation Charges (Rs/hec)	Mechanisation Cost (Rs/hec)	Human Labour Cost (Rs/hec)	Total cost (Rs/hec)	Gross Returns (Rs/hec)	Net Returns (Rs/hec)
Central Region	Gujarat	Bhavnagar	Small	3816.43	4233.91	0.00	3267.58	0.00	2216.50	3555.02	3502.29	18840.07	39431.80	105686.16	66254.36
			Medium	2539.80	4656.51	0.00	3201.45	0.00	2812.45	2879.42	2742.61	16359.83	35192.08	120195.51	85003.43
			Large	3088.36	4080.87	0.00	3841.82	0.00	2882.48	2832.23	3405.68	16347.10	36478.54	94518.31	58039.77
			District Average	2863.13	4466.87	0.00	3346.50	0.00	2729.89	2979.77	3005.59	16761.87	36153.61	112444.43	76290.82
		Surendranagar	Small	4776.01	3278.61	0.00	2847.64	0.00	2932.81	3937.57	3658.38	17321.90	3S752.91	139178.74	100425.83
			Medium	2558.67	2706.10	0.00	1915.43	0.00	3061.05	2507.47	2054.92	16781.48	31585.13	134272.81	102687.68
			Large	2300.81	2593.50	0.00	568.10	0.00	2758.35	2699.58	1794.87	14807.65	27522.86	149126.25	121603.39
			District Average	3331.06	2S98.28	0.00	2044.94	0.00	2966.33	3062.11	2601.88	16668.61	33573.20	138412.19	104838.99
		Gujarat Average		3038.90	3877.64	0.00	2857.58	0.00	2818.71	3010.70	2853.94	16726.84	35184.30	122198.97	87014.67
	Madhya Pradesh	Dhar	Small	2692.08	2558.95	0.00	3407.10	0.00	1829.15	1816.21	2090.82	17687.64	32081.94	69380.80	37298.86
			Medium	2666.14	3015.63	0.00	1139.62	24.18	1942.67	889.13	2165.26	15443.35	27285.98	63400.14	36114.16
			Large	1935.06	3025.64	0.00	455.96	0.00	2309.11	529.68	895.20	14102.58	23253.22	60212.13	36958.91
			District Average	2272.64	2991.22	0.00	918.11	9.53	2133.34	755.36	1473.85	14865.12	25419.17	62067.33	36648.15
		Khargone	Small	3323.42	2474.67	0.00	4370.00	0.00	1887.65	1805.73	2241.56	13772.42	29875.43	81000.96	51125.52
			Medium	2543.43	2713.55	48.14	1042.21	0.00	2478.60	967.09	1632.21	12452.93	23878.16	83989.48	60111.32
			Large	2183.41	2361.70	0.00	1548.05	0.00	2212.33	768.34	1220.62	12966.75	23261.20	78442.72	55181.52
			District Average	2411.30	2513.64	19.70	1540.55	0.00	2298.32	922.99	1461.18	12813.47	23981.15	80893.02	56911.87
		Madhya Pradesh Average		2337.28	2768.57	9.18	1208.30	5.09	2210.25	833.51	1467.95	13908.64	24748.77	70843.90	46095.14
	Maha–rashtra	Jalgaon	Small	2717.49	2719.81	271.17	4010.38	872.92	1705.16	1385.54	2440.80	13296.43	29419.69	74279.20	44859.51
			Medium	2982.75	2711.75	455.70	2409.90	569.16	2048.61	940.87	1952.14	13069.07	27139.94	62608.98	35469.04
			Large	3509.06	1850.84	0.00	3294.13	0.00	1611.98	731.50	1844.58	10794.09	23636.18	49306.12	25669.94
			District Average	3092.71	2400.63	232.82	3225.32	455.46	1783.69	1001.66	2063.58	12310.44	26566.30	61360.23	34793.93
		Yavatmal	Small	2428.16	2979.24	349.19	4663.36	1047.22	2095.45	1116.10	1242.44	14701.06	30622.21	78675.20	48052.99
			Medium	2330.49	4114.30	1265.47	2446.34	1071.24	2828.68	556.66	1334.60	15203.59	31151.38	85626.41	54475.03
			Large	2223.00	3501.07	421.80	4468.17	991.17	2676.45	507.30	1840.21	14195.04	30824.20	97532.81	66708.61

(*Contd.*)

Table 4.8 (*Contd.*)

Regions	States	Districts	Farm Size Categories	Seed Cost (Rs/hec)	Fertilizer Cost (Rs/hec)	Growth Regulators Cost (Rs/hec)	FYM Cost (Rs/hec)	Micro-nutrient Cost (Rs/hec)	Pesticide Cost (Rs/hec)	Irrigation Charges (Rs/hec)	Mechanisation Cost (Rs/hec)	Human Labour Cost (Rs/hec)	Total cost (Rs/hec)	Gross Returns (Rs/hec)	Net Returns (Rs/hec)
			District Average	2329.24	3476.19	628.20	3981.45	1034.23	2501.94	747.96	1477.41	14662.81	30839.43	87206.60	56367.17
		Maharashtra Average		2715.88	2931.49	427.97	3598.52	741.12	2138.20	876.44	1774.26	13471.50	28675.39	74117.22	45441.83
Southern Region	Andhra Pradesh	Adilabad	Small	2303.59	4232.65	0.00	0.00	182.05	2074.05	606.98	2812.51	19521.00	31732.84	72148.60	40415.76
			Medium	2488.72	3960.20	0.00	0.00	50.33	1764.43	480.42	2724.10	22986.08	34454.29	75835.73	41381.44
			Large	2084.97	4162.68	0.00	0.00	363.24	2373.23	224.09	2324.71	21503.53	33036.44	69624.94	36588.50
			District Average	2378.17	4064.81	0.00	0.00	132.79	1939.47	477.05	2689.07	21817.75	33499.10	73905.37	40406.28
		Warangal	Small	2511.64	3276.98	106.00	1308.08	422.98	3191.52	529.66	2945.96	22180.13	36472.95	137838.68	101365.74
			Medium	2244.44	347122	119.97	1888.63	428.13	2675 77	413.69	2781.69	21321.81	35345.35	164184.43	128839.08
			Large	2113.22	3377.54	0.00	5488.89	1097.78	1697.99	180.49	2085.78	10808.61	26850.29	135026.67	108176.38
			District Average	2397.21	3345.64	102.24	1811.39	476.44	2914.99	466.45	2828.35	21037.26	35379.96	145887.32	110507.36
		Andhra Pradesh Average		2384.61	3821.59	34.58	612.60	249.01	2269.38	473.46	2736.17	21553.79	34135.19	98249.15	64113.96
	Karnataka	Dharwad	Small	2764.64	3039.20	0.00	1487.51	77.19	2058.47	315.23	1892.34	14421.74	26056.32	86579.56	60523.25
			Medium	3098.82	3109.46	0.00	1296.75	0.00	2410.31	316.50	1690.77	11487.92	23410.52	112182.60	88772.07
			Large	2429.86	2941.36	0.00	1080.63	0.00	1672.19	115.88	1216.15	6807.62	16263.69	159932.50	143668.81
			District Average	2858.16	3056.67	0.00	1386.29	43.23	2154.23	299.74	1765.68	12756.44	24320.42	101664.89	77344.47
		Karnataka Average		2858.16	3056.67	0.00	1386.29	43.23	2154.23	299.74	1765.68	12756.44	24320.42	101664.89	77344.47
	Tamil Nadu	Virudunagar	Small	2504.97	4870.77	0.00	0.00	0.00	1971.41	1454.52	3851.75	19481.66	34135.09	78116.82	43981.73
			Medium	2692.70	4585.68	0.00	91.11	0.00	177738	1289.99	3849.42	18476.41	32762.69	88002.86	55240.17
			Large	0.00	0.00	0.00	0.00	0.00	0.00	0.00	0.00	0.00	0.00	0.00	0.00
			District Average	2574.52	4765.15	0.00	33. 75	0.00	1899.53	1393.56	3850.89	19109.23	33626.64	81779.43	48152.79
		Tamil Nadu Average		2574.52	4765.15	0.00	33.75	0.00	1899.53	1393.56	3850.89	19109.23	33626.64	81779.43	48152.79
All India			Small	2979.81	3261.21	80.60	1748.02	365.03	2391.50	1490.64	3008.93	17427.17	32752.92	96340.36	63587.44
			Medium	2948.39	3346.51	113.86	928.42	299.11	2779.23	1061.69	2877.12	15610.54	29964.86	100265.78	70300.92
			Large	2569.14	2939.08	59.54	1282.45	217.49	2577.47	814.97	1962.35	14110.94	26533.43	85949.37	59415.94
			All India Average	2834.25	3197.05	39.00	1226.40	287.89	2627.30	1079.56	2614.45	15540.88	29496.78	94804.60	65307.82

Source: Primary field survey

was the highest (₹ 145887.32/hec), though the average of Andhra Pradesh was relatively low at ₹ 98249.12/hec. The lowest gross returns were seen for Maharashtra (₹ 74117.22/hec) followed by Madhya Pradesh (₹ 70843.90/hec). The per-hectare value of output is observed to be scale neutral across farm size categories.

As regards net returns per hectare it is found to be positive in all the regions indicating profits to farmers from cultivation of Bt cotton. The average net returns from Bt cotton at the all India level was ₹ 65307.82/hec. The highest net returns per hectare were seen in the Hanumangarh district of Rajasthan (₹ 110946.42/hec). This was followed by Gujarat (₹ 87014.67/hec) wherein the contribution of Surendranagar was ₹ 104838.99/hec. The net returns from Warangal district of Andhra Pradesh was also very high (₹ 110507.36/hec), though the average of Andhra Pradesh was relatively low at ₹ 64113.96/hec. The lowest net returns were seen for Madhya Pradesh (₹ 46095.14/hec) followed by Maharashtra (₹ 45441.83/hec). The per hectare net returns are seen to be scale neutral across farm size classes. In the field study, it was further found that the total income or net returns from Bt cotton was much higher than income from other crops of non-farm sources.

Table 4.9: Proportion of Farm Cost to Total Cost (%)

Districts	*Seed Cost (Rs/ha)*	*Fertilizer Cost (Rs/ha)*	*Growth Regulators Cost (Rs/ha)*	*FYM Cost (Rs/ha)*	*Micro-nutrient Cost (Rs/ha)*	*Pesticide Cost (Rs/ha)*	*Irrigation Charges (Rs/ha)*	*Mechanisation Cost (Rs/ha)*	*Human Labour Cost (Rs/ha)*
Bhatinda	11.08	10.37	0.04	0.03	1.49	11.02	0.79	14.25	50.93
Fazilka	14.44	9.43	0.83	1.08	2.54	13.98	1.10	14.21	42.39
Punjab	**12.67**	**9.92**	**0.42**	**0.53**	**1.99**	**12.42**	**0.93**	**14.23**	**46.89**
Hissar	10.73	10.99	0.00	0.58	0.27	9.93	6.84	10.17	50.49
Sirsa	7.87	7.49	0.12	0.41	1.11	7.29	5.60	6.78	63.32
Haryana	**9.33**	**9.28**	**0.06**	**0.50**	**0.68**	**8.64**	**6.23**	**8.52**	**56.76**
Hanumangarh	8.28	13.75	0.20	0.00	2.42	9.58	2.48	12.35	50.94
Rajasthan	**8.28**	**13.75**	**0.20**	**0.00**	**2.42**	**9.58**	**2.48**	**12.35**	**50.94**
Bhavnagar	7.92	12.36	0.00	9.26	0.00	7.55	8.24	8.31	46.36
Surendranagar	9.92	8.63	0.00	6.09	0.00	8.84	9.12	7.75	49.65
Gujarat	**8.64**	**11.02**	**0.00**	**8.12**	**0.00**	**8.01**	**8.56**	**8.11**	**47.54**
Dhar	8.94	11.77	0.00	3.61	0.04	8.39	2.97	5.80	58.48
Khargone	10.05	10.48	0.08	6.42	0.00	9.58	3.85	6.09	53.43
Madhya Pradesh	**9.44**	**11.19**	**0.04**	**4.88**	**0.02**	**8.93**	**3.37**	**5.93**	**56.20**
Jalgaon	11.64	9.04	0.88	12.14	1.71	6.71	3.77	7.77	46.34
Yavatmal	7.55	11.27	2.04	12.91	3.35	8.11	2.43	4.79	47.55
Maharashtra	**9.47**	**10.22**	**1.49**	**12.55**	**2.58**	**7.46**	**3.06**	**6.19**	**46.98**
Adilabad	7.10	12.13	0.00	0.00	0.40	5.79	1.42	8.03	65.13
Warangal	6.78	9.46	0.29	5.12	1.35	8.24	1.32	7.99	59.46
Andhra Pradesh	**6.99**	**11.20**	**0.10**	**1.79**	**0.73**	**6.65**	**1.39**	**8.02**	**63.14**
Dharwad	11.75	12.57	0.00	5.70	0.18	8.86	1.23	7.26	52.45
Karnataka	**11.75**	**12.57**	**0.00**	**5.70**	**0.18**	**8.86**	**1.23**	**7.26**	**52.45**
Virudunagar	7.66	14.17	0.00	0.10	0.00	5.65	4.14	11.45	56.83
Tamil Nadu	**7.66**	**14.17**	**0.00**	**0.10**	**0.00**	**5.65**	**4.14**	**11.45**	**56.83**
India	**9.61**	**10.84**	**0.30**	**4.16**	**0.98**	**8.91**	**3.66**	**8.86**	**52.69**

Source: Primary Field Survey.

It is seen from the Table 4.9 that the share of human labour costs in total costs from cultivation of Bt cotton is the highest (around 50%) in all the districts. In the State of Punjab, after human labour costs taking up 47 per cent of total costs, cost of mechanization (14.23%), seed (12.67%) and pesticide (12.42%) are high. In Haryana, after human labour costs occupying 57 per cent of total costs, costs of seed (9.33%) are followed by fertilizer (9.28%). The share of pesticide cost (8.64%) and mechanization cost (8.52%) are similar. In Rajasthan, after human labour costs taking up 51 per cent of total costs, cost of fertilizer (13.75%) and mechanisation (12.35%) are high. In the State of Gujarat, after human labour costs taking up 48 per cent of total costs, cost of fertilizer (11.02%) is the highest. These are followed very closely with costs of seed, irrigation, farmyard manure, mechanization and pesticide (around 8%). In case of Madhya Pradesh, the human labour costs were around 56.20 per cent. This was followed by cost of fertilizer (11.19%), seed (9.44%) and pesticide (8.93%). In case of Maharashtra, the human labour costs were around 47 per cent. This was followed by cost of farmyard manure (12.55%), fertilizer (10.22%) seed cost (9.47%) and lastly pesticide cost (7.46%). In the State of Andhra Pradesh the share of human labour cost to total cost was 63.14 per cent. This was followed by cost of fertilizer (11.20%) and that of mechanization (8.02%). In Karnataka, the share of human labour cost to total cost was 52.45 per cent. This was followed mainly by cost of fertilizer (12.57%) and that of seed (11.75%). In Tamil Nadu, the share of human labour cost to total cost was 57 per cent. This was followed mainly by cost of fertilizer (14.17%) and mechanization cost (11.45%). Overall it was seen that the highest proportional input cost in the total cost was that of fertilizers (10.84%), followed by that of seed (9.61%). Pesticide and mechanization cost was 8.91 and 8.86 per cent of the total cost. Cost of farmyard manure and irrigation formed 4.16 and 3.66 per cent of the total cost. The proportional cost of micronutrients and growth regulators was very less 0.98 and 0.30 per cent only. Among micronutrients it was seen that sample farmers in Rajasthan and Maharashtra had used micronutrients and it formed slightly more than 2 per cent of total cost. Growth regulators were used by sample farmers in Maharashtra and it formed 1.49 per cent of the total cost.

It may be further seen that the average per hectare cost of cultivation increased by 67.68 per cent in the Post-Bt cotton period from the Pre-Bt cotton period as per the data provided by the Directorate of Economics and Statistics, Ministry of Agriculture, Government of India (Table 4.10). The growth rates also confirm this increase. This means that the cost of cultivation of Bt cotton is greater than Non-Bt cotton, that was cultivated in India prior to the advent of Bt cotton in 2002-03. The per hectare cost of cultivation showed further increase in the latest 3 years of available data (2006-07 to 2008-09) in all the States. As observed from the field survey (Table 4.9), high costs in Bt cotton were mainly due to costs of human labour (52.69% of total cost) followed by fertilizers (10.84%), seed (9.61%) and mechanization (8.86%).

Table 4.10: Cost of Cultivation (Cost C2*) of Cotton (₹/hec)

States	*Average Cost of Cultivation (Rs/hec)*		*% Change*	*Growth Rates (%)*		*2006-07 to 2008-09 Avg (Rs/hec)*
	Pre-Bt Cotton Period (1996-01)	*Post-Bt Cotton Period (2002-08)*		*1996-2001*	*2002-09*	
Andhra Pradesh	21825.94	35067.46	60.67	–1.91	5.88	40021.06
Gujarat	14839.28	27473.16	85.14	1.85	13.63	32799.56
Haryana	18716.10	33853.11	80.88	7.17	17.98	36224.79
Madhya Pradesh	9966.76	25680.99	157.67	–1.45	8.71	28878.96
Karnataka	10393.57	15045.83	44.76	4.67	10.73	18888.47
Maharashtra	13938.44	23314.51	67.27	7.15	6.17	26384.99
Punjab	24369.08	40508.69	66.23	10.97	14.04	42728.43
Rajasthan	14603.15	26210.32	79.48	4.08	18.97	29082.39
Tamil Nadu	26036.26	31467.35	20.86	7.38	1.76	32816.12
India	16348.70	27412.70	67.68	3.98	8.45	31980.53

* Cost C2 includes variable and fixed costs of cultivation.

Source: Directorate of Economics and Statistics, Ministry of Agriculture and Cooperation.

Table 4.11shows that the average per hectare value of production increased by 94.06 per cent in the Post-Bt cotton period from the Pre-Bt cotton period. The growth rates also confirm this increase. The per hectare value of production showed further increase in the latest 3 years of available data (2006-07 to 2008-09) in all the States. Further, the percentage change and growth rates in the value of production from the Pre-Bt cotton to the Post Bt-cotton period is found to be more than those

Table 4.11: Value of Production of Cotton (₹/hec)

States	*Average Value of Production (Rs/hec)*		*% Change*	*Growth Rates (%)*		*2006-07 to 2008-09 Average (Rs/hec)*
	Pre-Bt Cotton Period (1996-2001)	*Post-Bt Cotton Period (2002-2008)*		*1996-2001*	*2002-2009*	
Andhra Pradesh	22653.14	40650.64	79.45	1.29	4.97	47809.28
Gujarat	17182.47	37543.21	118.50	–11.67	15.37	45566.97
Haryana	19609.36	39462.68	101.24	8.15	37.94	44724.72
Madhya Pradesh	9610.36	26883.46	179.73	–2.74	21.49	33882.53
Karnataka	9910.38	18138.80	83.03	–2.05	10.12	23357.00
Maharashtra	13138.39	23118.63	75.96	2.25	8.77	27527.71
Punjab	22096.63	50883.50	130.28	16.77	19.83	54526.92
Rajasthan	20173.44	36882.52	82.83	2.67	19.06	40760.36
Tamil Nadu	23063.29	29704.46	28.80	3.62	8.52	36245.19
India	16291.27	31614.66	94.06	0.11	12.49	39377.85

Source: Directorate of Economics and Statistics, Ministry of Agriculture and Cooperation.

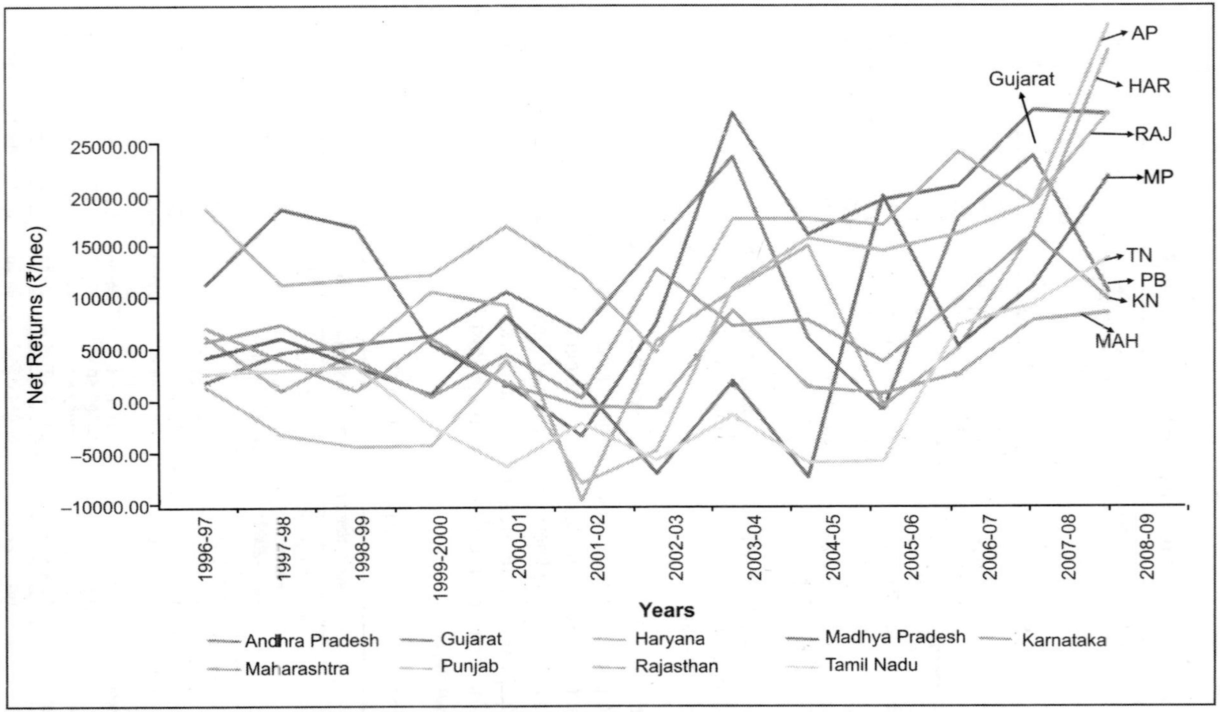

Source: Directorate of Economics and Statistics, Ministry of Agriculture and Cooperation

Fig. 4.1: Net Returns from Cotton Cultivation (₹/hec)

of cost of cultivation of Bt cotton. This shows that despite high cost of cultivation farmers are deriving greater benefits from Bt cotton cultivation.

Table 4.12: Average Net Returns (₹ /hec)

States	*Pre-Bt Cotton Period (1996-2001)*	*Post-Bt Cotton Period (2002-2008)*	*% Change*	*2006-07 to 2008-09 Average (Rs/hec)*
Andhra Pradesh	827.20	5583.18	574.95	7788.22
Gujarat	2343.19	10070.04	329.76	12767.40
Haryana	893.25	5609.57	527.99	8499.93
Madhya Pradesh	–356.40	1202.47	437.39	5003.58
Karnataka	–483.19	3092.97	740.12	4468.53
Maharashtra	–800.05	–195.87	75.52	1142.73
Punjab	–2272.45	10374.81	556.55	11798.49
Rajasthan	5570.30	10672.20	91.59	11677.97
Tamil Nadu	–2972.97	–1762.89	40.70	3429.07
India	**305.43**	**4960.72**	**374.95**	**7397.32**

Source: Directorate of Economics and Statistics, Ministry of Agriculture and Cooperation.

As regards net returns per hectare, it is seen that since 2002-03 the net returns from Bt cotton showed general increase, despite severe fluctuations (Figure 4.1). The average net returns per hectare also changed significantly by 374.95 per cent from the Pre to the Post-Bt cotton period. This change was much greater than the increased costs of Bt cotton cultivation (Table 4.12). The per hectare net returns showed further increase in the latest 3 years of available data (2006-07 to 2008-09) in all the States. Hence, it can be safely said that net returns from Bt cotton are much higher than the increase in its cost of cultivation. However, it also needs to be pointed out that amongst all States, the net returns per hectare is the least in Maharashtra (₹ 1143/hec).

5

Factors Influencing Bt Cotton Yields

Productivity Functions

In this study a productivity function using the Cobb Douglas method was used. This function was used in order to know the contribution of a particular input in the total agricultural productivity. In this function the variables estimated in their unrestricted form are expressed in logarithms so as to introduce linearity. Thus, this model is also known as Log Linear Model. The Cobb Douglas productivity framework has been used in this study to estimate the output elasticities of different variables. The value of elasticity measures the per cent change in Bt cotton productivity with 1 per cent change in explanatory variable. Each factor's (input) contribution in the total productivity function can be measured, holding other inputs constant. The ordinary least squares (OLS) estimates of Bt cotton productivity (Cobb Douglas) are presented in Table 5.1. In this function the per hectare gross value of output from Bt cotton productivity (independent variable) has been regressed on net cultivated area, per hectare seed, fertilizer, farmyard manure, growth regulator, pesticide, irrigation, human labour and machine labour costs (dependent variables).

At the all India level it is seen that per hectare cost of fertilizers, micronutrients, pesticides, irrigation and mechanization have a positive and statistically significant relationship at 1 per cent level of significance with the productivity of Bt cotton. Net cultivated area, per hectare cost of seed, growth regulators and labour costs show a negative though statistically non-significant relationship with the productivity of Bt cotton. In the case of Bt cotton seed that shows a negative yet statistically non-significant relationship with productivity, it may be said that the huge proliferation in hybrid Bt seeds in the recent years are compromising on quality parameters.

Table 5.1: Productivity Function (Cobb Douglas Method)

Regions	*States*	*Districts*	*NCA*	*Seed Cost*	*Fertilizer Cost*	*Growth Regulators Cost*	*FYM Cost*	*Micro-nutrient Cost*	*Pesticide Cost*	*Irrigation Cost*	*Mechani-zation Cost*	*Labour Cost*
Northern Region	Punjab	Bathinda	–0.047	0.036	0.142	0.037***	0.017	0.013	0.082	–0.071	–0.026	0.054
		Fazilka	0.012	0.805***	–0.044	–0.008	–0.017*	0.025*	0.046	–0.057	–0.051	0.023
	Haryana	Hissar	–0.024	–0.116	0.080		0.003	0.017	0.286***	–0.001	0.065	–0.044
		Sirsa	0.036	–0.045	0.169	0.005	0.000	0.023**	–0.116	–0.060	0.008	0.123*
	Rajasthan	Hanumangarh	–0.050	–0.229*	0.166**	0.069***		–0.006	0.010	0.041	–0.164**	–0.026
Central Region	Gujarat	Bhavnagar	–0.036	–0.001	–0.093		–0.008		0.041	–0.068	–0.087	0.259***
		Surendranagar	–0.023	–0.308**	0.111		0.008		–0.101	0.100	0.096	0.140
	Madhya Pradesh	Dhar	0.124*	0.137	0.125		0.024	–0.023	–0.153	0.219**	0.036	–0.024
		Khargone	–0.005	0.117	0.063	–0.051*	0.020		0.098	–0.012	–0.060	–0.179
	Maharashtra	Jalgaon	–0.131	0.023	0.133	0.034	0.001	0.005	–0.083	0.057	–0.190	–0.103
		Yavatmal	0.142	0.041	0.053	0.014	0.016	0.008	–0.058	0.152	0.088	–0.092
Southern Region	Andhra Pradesh	Adilabad	0.062	–0.156	–0.110			0.004	0.209**	–0.021	0.109	0.072
		Warangal	0.164***	0.148	–0.127	0.024	0.025**	–0.007	0.024	0.220**	–0.110	–0.021
	Karnataka	Dharwad	0.107	–0.045	–0.044		0.032**	–0.041	–0.096	–0.178	0.069	–0.010
	Tamil Nadu	Virudunagar	0.114	0.150*	0.034		0.020		–0.077*	–0.059	–0.414***	0.046
All India			–0.003	–0.03	0.08***	–0.02	0.001	0.021***	0.119***	0.035***	0.122***	–0.03

Source: Primary Field Survey.

*** Statistically significant at 1% level of significance

** Statistically significant at 5% level of significance

* Statistically significant at 10% level of significance

At the district level, it is found that farm size and Bt cotton productivity show a negative though statistically non-significant relationship in the districts of Bathinda in Punjab, Hissar in Haryana, Hanumangarh in Rajasthan, Bhavnagar and Surendranagar in Gujarat, Khargone in Madhya Pradesh and Jalgaon in Maharashtra. Farm size and Bt cotton productivity show a positive though statistically non-significant relationship in the districts of Fazilka in Punjab, Sirsa in Haryana, Yavatmal in Maharashtra, Adilabad in Andhra Pradesh, Dharwad in Karnataka and Virudunagar in Tamil Nadu. However, the relationship is found to be statistically significant at 1 per cent level of significance only in the district of Warangal in Andhra Pradesh and at 5 per cent level of significance in the district of Dhar in Madhya Pradesh.

Per hectare seed costs show a significantly positive relationship at 1 per cent level of significance with Bt cotton productivity in the districts of Fazilka in Punjab and at 10 per cent level in the district of Virudunagar in Tamil Nadu. In the districts of Bathinda in Punjab, Dhar and Khargone in Madhya Pradesh and Jalgaon and Yavatmal in Maharashtra, the relationship was found to be positive but not statistically significant. The relationship was found to be significantly negative at 1 per cent level of significance in the Surendranagar district of Gujarat and at 10 per cent level of significance in the Hanumangarh district of Rajasthan. This significant negative relationship between seed costs and productivity could be attributed to unavailability of high yielding quality of Bt cotton seeds that are significantly affecting its yields in the Hanumangarh district of Rajasthan and Surendranagar district of Gujarat.

Per hectare fertilizer costs show a significantly positive relationship at 5 per cent level of significance with Bt cotton productivity in the Hanumangarh district of Rajasthan. The relationship was positive though statistically insignificant in the Bathinda district of Punjab, Hissar and Sirsa district of Haryana, Surendranagar district of Gujarat, Dhar and Khargone districts of Madhya Pradesh, Jalgaon and Yavatmal districts of Maharashtra, and Virudunagar district of Tamil Nadu. The relationship was positive though statistically insignificant in the Fazilka district of Punjab, Bhavnagar district of Gujarat, Adilabad and Warangal district of Andhra Pradesh and Dharwad district of Karnataka.

Growth regulators were not used in several regions and it showed a significantly positive relationship at 1 per cent level of significance in the Bathinda district of Punjab and Hanumangarh district of Rajasthan. It showed a significantly negative relationship at 10 per cent level of significance with Bt cotton productivity in the Khargone district of Madhya Pradesh and a non-significant negative relationship in the Fazilka district of Punjab. In the district of Sirsa in Haryana, Jalgaon and Yavatmal in Maharashtra and Warangal in Andhra Pradesh, the relationship was positive yet non-significant. Improper applications of growth regulators are significantly affecting Bt cotton yields in the Khargone district of Madhya Pradesh. Hence, balanced application of growth regulators is needed in this region.

The relationship between farmyard manure and Bt cotton productivity showed a significantly positive relationship at 5 per cent level of significance in the Warangal district of Andhra Pradesh and Dharwad district of Karnataka. However, in the districts of Bathinda in Punjab, Hissar and Sirsa in Haryana, Surendranagar in Gujarat, Dhar and Khargone in Madhya Pradesh, Jalgaon and Yavatmal in Maharashtra and Virudunagar in Tamil Nadu, the relationship was positive yet non-significant. Only in the district of Fazilka in Punjab, the relationship was negative and statistically significant at 5 per cent level of significance. Farmyard manure was not used by sample farmers in the remaining districts Hanumangarh in Rajasthan and Adilabad in Andhra Pradesh. Improper applications of farmyard manure are significantly affecting Bt cotton yields in the Fazilka district of Punjab. Hence, balanced application of farmyard manure is needed in this region.

Micronutrients were not used by farmers in the survey districts of Gujarat, Khargone district of Madhya Pradesh and Virudunagar district of Tamil Nadu. It showed a significantly positive relation at 5 per cent level of significance with Bt cotton productivity in the Sirsa district of Haryana and at 10 per cent level of significance in the Fazilka district of Punjab. In the Bathinda district of Punjab, Hissar district of Haryana, Jalgaon and Yavatmal districts of Haryana as well as the Adilabad district of Andhra Pradesh, the relationship was positive but not significant. In the Hanumangarh district of Rajasthan, Dhar district of Madhya Pradesh, Warangal district of Andhra Pradesh and Dharwad district of Karnataka, the relationship was negative though not statistically significant.

Per hectare pesticide use showed a positive relationship at 1 per cent level of significance with Bt cotton productivity in the Sirsa district of Haryana, and at 10 per cent level of significance in the Adilabad district of Andhra Pradesh. In the survey districts of Punjab, Hanumangarh in Rajasthan, Bhavnagar in Gujarat, Khargone in Madhya Pradesh and Warangal in Andhra Pradesh, the relationship was positive yet insignificant. In the survey districts of Virudunagar in Tamil Nadu the relationship was negative and statistically significant at 10 per cent level of significance, while in the districts of Sirsa in Haryana, Surendranagar in Gujarat, Dhar in Madhya Pradesh, Maharashtra districts as well as Dharwad in Karnataka, the relationship was negative yet not statistically significant.

As regards irrigation, it was found that per hectare charges for irrigation showed a statistically significant positive relationship at 5 per cent level of significance with the productivity of Bt cotton in the Dhar district of Madhya Pradesh and the Warangal district of Andhra Pradesh. In the districts of Hanumangarh in Rajasthan, Surendranagar in Gujarat, and survey districts of

Maharashtra, the relationship was positive though statistically non-significant. However, the relationship was negative but statistically non-significant in the survey districts of Punjab and Haryana, Bhavnagar district of Gujarat, Khargone in Madhya Pradesh, Adilabad in Andhra Pradesh, Dharwad in Karnataka and Virudunagar in Tamil Nadu.

Per hectare charges of mechanisation showed a significant negative relationship at 1 per cent level of significance with Bt cotton productivity in the districts of Hanumangarh in Rajasthan and Virudunagar in Tamil Nadu. A negative though non-significant relationship was also seen in the survey districts of Punjab, Bhavnagar in Gujarat, Khargone in Madhya Pradesh, Jalgaon in Maharashtra and Warangal in Andhra Pradesh. A positive though non-significant relationship was seen in the survey districts of Haryana, Surendranagar district of Gujarat, Dhar in Madhya Pradesh, Yavatmal in Maharashtra, Adilabad in Andhra Pradesh and Dharwad in Karnataka. Improper methods and techniques of mechanization in Bt cotton fields are significantly affecting Bt cotton yields in the Hanumangarh district of Rajasthan and Virudunagar district of Tamil Nadu. Hence mechanization techniques need to be properly executed in these regions.

The relationship between per hectare costs of human labour and Bt cotton productivity was positive and statistically significant at 1 per cent level of significance in the Bhavnagar district of Gujarat and also positively significant at 10 per cent level of significance in the Sirsa district of Haryana. The relationship was positive yet non-significant in the selected survey districts of Punjab, Surendranagar in Gujarat, Adilabad in Andhra Pradesh and Virudunagar in Tamil Nadu. The relationship was negative yet non-significant in the selected survey districts of Hissar in Haryana and Maharashtra, Hanumangarh in Rajasthan, Dhar and Khargone in Madhya Pradesh, Warangal in Andhra Pradesh and Dharwad in Karnataka.

The results of productivity function show that several factors which resulted in improper crop management and farming practices which affected cotton productivity. Unavailability of high yielding quality of Bt cotton seeds seemed to be significantly affecting Bt cotton yields in the Hanumangarh district of Rajasthan and Surendranagar district of Gujarat. Improper applications of growth regulators were significantly affecting Bt cotton yields in the Khargone district of Madhya Pradesh. Hence, balanced application of growth regulators was needed in this region. Improper applications of farmyard manure were significantly affecting Bt cotton yields in the Fazilka district of Punjab. Hence, balanced application of farmyard manure was needed in this district. Improper methods and techniques of mechanization in Bt cotton fields were significantly affecting Bt cotton yields in the Hanumangarh district of

Rajasthan and Virudunagar district of Tamil Nadu. Hence, mechanization techniques needed to be properly improved and executed in these regions.

PRODUCTIVITY FUNCTIONS : REGRESSIONS

Northern Region

Punjab

Bathinda

Regression Statistics	
Multiple R	0.58
R Square	0.34
Adjusted R Square	0.23
Standard Error	0.12
Observations	70

	Coefficients	*Standard Error*	*t Stat*	*P-value*
Intercept	8.83	0.97	9.06	0.00
NV-NCA	–0.05	0.04	–1.31	0.20
Bt-LN-Seed Cost	0.04	0.04	0.87	0.39
Bt-LN-Fertilizer Cost	0.14	0.11	1.30	0.20
Bt-LN-Cost of Growth Regulators	0.04	0.01	3.02	0.00
Bt-LN-Cost of FYM	0.02	0.02	1.03	0.31
Bt-LN-Cost of Micronutrient	0.01	0.01	1.65	0.10
Bt-LN-Pesticide Cost	0.08	0.05	1.65	0.10
Bt-LN-Irrigation Charges	–0.07	0.04	–1.66	0.10
Bt-LN-Mechanization Cost	-0.03	0.07	–0.36	0.72
Bt-LN-Labour Cost	0.05	0.04	1.44	0.16

Fazilka

Regression Statistics	
Multiple R	0.52
R Square	0.27
Adjusted R Square	0.15
Standard Error	0.19
Observations	70

	Coefficients	*Standard Error*	*t Stat*	*P-value*
Intercept	5.08	2.23	2.27	0.03
LN-NCA	0.01	0.05	0.25	0.81
Bt-LN-Seed Cost	0.81	0.27	2.93	0.00
Bt-LN-Fertilizer Cost	–0.84	0.11	–0.40	0.69
Bt-LN-Cost of Growth Regulates	–0.01	0.01	–0.58	0.57
Bt-LN-Cost of FVM	–0.02	0.01	–1.98	0.05
Bt-LN-Cost of Micronutrient	0.03	0.01	1.95	0.06
Bt-LN-Pesticide Cost	0.05	0.07	0.62	0.34
Bt-LN-Irrigation Cost	–0.06	0.07	–0.87	0.39
Bt-LN-Mechanization Cost	–0.05	0.12	–0.42	0.57
Bt-LN Labour Cost	0.02	0.07	0.34	0.73

Haryana

Hissar

Regression Statistics	
Multiple R	0.58
R Square	0.34
Adjusted R Square	0.24
Standard Error	0.25
Observations	70

	Coefficients	*Standard Error*	*t Stat*	*P-value*
Intercept	8.92	1.80	4.95	0.00
LN-NCA	–0.02	0.05	–0.45	0.65
Bt-LN-Seed Cost	–0.12	0.10	–1.16	0.25
Bt-LN-Fertilizer Cost	0.08	0.13	0.60	0.55
Bt-LN-Cost of FYM	0.00	0.02	0.15	0.88
Bt-LN-Cost of Micronutrient	0.02	0.02	0.93	0.35
Bt-LN Pesticide Cost	0.29	0.06	4.54	0.00
Bt-LN-Irrigation Charges	0.00	0.12	–0.01	0.99
Bt- LN-Mechanization Cost	0.06	0.08	0.78	0.44
Bt-LN-Labour Cost	–0.04	0.09	–0.47	0.64

Sirsa

Regression Statistics	
Multiple R	0.58
R Square	0.33
Adjusted R Square	0.22
Standard Error	0.21
Observations	70

	Coefficients	*Standard Error*	*t Stat*	*P-value*
Intercept	9.60	1.17	8.18	0.00
LN-NCA	0.04	0.04	0.85	0.40
Bt-LN-Seed Cost	–0.04	0.07	–0.64	0.52
Bt- LN-Fertilizer Cost	0.17	0.11	1.48	0.14
Bt-LN-Cost of Growth Regulator	0.00	0.03	0.16	0.88
Bt-LN-Cost of FYM	0.00	0.03	0.01	0.99
Bt-LN-Cost of Micronutrient	0.02	0.01	2.25	0.03
Bt-LN-Pesticide Cost	–0.12	0.08	–1.48	0.14
Bt-LM-Irrigation Charges	–0.06	0.07	–0.86	0.39
Bt- LN-Mechanization Cost	0.01	0.07	0.13	0.90
Bt-LN-Labour Cost	0.12	0.07	1.88	0.07

Rajasthan

Hanumangarh

Regression Statistics	
Multiple R	0.50
R Square	0.25
Adjusted R Square	0.14
Standard Error	0.18
Observations	70

	Coefficients	*Standard Error*	*t Stat*	*P-value*
Intercept	12.40	1.18	10.48	0.00
LN-NCA	–0.05	0.03	–1.58	0.12
Bt-LN-Seed Cost	–0.23	0.13	–1.72	0.09
Bt-LN-Fertilizer Cost	0.17	0.07	2.53	0.01
Bt-LN-Cost of Growth Regulators	0.07	0.02	2.85	0.01
Bt-LN-Cost of Micronutrient	–0.01	0.01	–0.72	0.47
Bt-LN-Pesticide Cost	0.01	0.05	0.18	0.86
Bt-LN-Irrigation Charges	0.04	0.07	0.56	0.58
Bt-LN-Mechanization Cost	–0.16	0.08	–2.06	0.04
Bt-LN-Labour Cost	–0.03	0.06	–0.44	0.66

Central Region

Gujarat

Bhavnagar

Regression Statistics	
Multiple R	0.39
R Square	0.15
Adjusted R Square	0.04
Standard Error	0.29
Observations	70

	Coefficients	*Standard Error*	*t Stat*	*P-value*
Intercept	10.03	1.77	5.67	0.00
LN-NCA	–0.04	0.05	–0.69	0.49
Bt-LN-Seed Cost	0.00	0.09	–0.02	0.99
Bt-LN-Fertilizer Cost	–0.09	0.14	–0.68	0.50
Bt-LN-Cost of FYM	–0.01	0.01	–0.73	0.47
Bt-LN-Pesticide Cost	0.04	0.07	0.57	0.57
Bt-LN-Irrigation Charges	–0.07	0.10	–0.68	0.50
Bt-LN-Mechanization Cost	–0.09	0.09	–1.00	0.32
Bt-LN-Labour Cost	0.26	0.10	2.70	0.01

Surendranagar

Regression Statistics	
Multiple R	0.39
R Square	0.15
Adjusted R Square	0.04
Standard Error	0.27
Observations	70

	Coefficients	*Standard Error*	*t Stat*	*P-value*
Intercept	10.45	1.49	6.99	0.00
LN-NCA	–0.02	0.05	–0.44	0.66
Bt-LN-Seed Cost	–0.31	0.12	–2.57	0.01
Bt-LN-Fertilizer Cost	0.11	0.10	1.12	0.27
Bt-LN-Cost of FYM	0.01	0.01	0.90	0.37
Bt-LN-Pesticide Cost	–0.10	0.07	–1.51	0.14
Bt-LN-Irrigation Charges	0.10	0.07	1.38	0.17
Bt-LN-Mechanization Cost	0.10	0.10	0.98	0.33
Bt-LN-Labour Cost	0.14	0.16	0.88	0.38

Madhya Pradesh

Dhar

Regression Statistics	
Multiple R	0.54
R Square	0.29
Adjusted R Square	0.19
Standard Error	0.23
Observations	70

	Coefficients	*Standard Error*	*t Stat*	*P-value*
Intercept	7.55	1.94	3.89	0.00
LN-NCA	0.12	0.06	1.99	0.05
Bt-LN-Seed Cost	0.14	0.10	1.36	0.18
Bt-LN Fertilizer Cost	0.13	0.10	1.25	0.21
Bt-LN-Cost of FYM	0.02	0.02	1.28	0.21
Bt-LN-Cost of Micronutrient	–0.02	0.05	–0.50	0.62
Bt-LN-Pesticide Cost	–0.15	0.09	–1.65	0.10
Bt-LN-Irrigation Charges	0.22	0.10	2.20	0.03
Bt-LN-Mechanization Cost	0.04	0.09	0.40	0.69
Bt-LN-Labour Cost	–0.02	0.15	–0.17	0.87

Khargone

Regression Statistics	
Multiple R	0.50
R Square	0.25
Adjusted R Square	0.14
Standard Error	0.18
Observations	70

	Coefficients	*Standard Error*	*t Stat*	*P-value*
Intercept	10.38	1.09	9.53	0.00
LN-NCA (Ac)	–0.01	0.03	–0.16	0.87
Bt-LN-Seed Cost	0.12	0.08	1.54	0.13
Bt-LN-Fertilizer Cost	0.06	0.09	0.67	0.51
Bt-LN-Cost of Growth Regulators	–0.05	0.03	–1.69	0.10
Bt-LN-Cost of FYM	0.02	0.01	1.59	0.12
Bt-LN-Pesticide Cost	0.10	0.08	1.22	0.23
Bt-LN-Irrigation Charges	–0.01	0.04	–0.27	0.79
Bt-LN-Mechanization Cost	–0.06	0.09	–0.67	0.51
Bt-LN-Labour Cost	–0.18	0.07	–1.10	0.01

Maharashtra

Jalgaon

Regression Statistics	
Multiple R	0.55
R Square	0.31
Adjusted R Square	0.19
Standard Error	0.27
Observations	70

	Coefficients	*Standard Error*	*t Stat*	*P-value*
Intercept	11.60	2.22	5.24	0.00
LN-NCA	–0.13	0.08	–1.65	0.11
Bt-LN-Seed Cost	0.02	0.11	0.21	0.84
Bt-LN-Fertilizer Cost	0.13	0.13	0.99	0.33
Bt-LN-Cost of Growth Regulators	0.03	0.03	1.31	0.20
Bt-LN-Cost of FYM	0.00	0.01	0.09	0.93
Bt-LN-Cost of Micronutrient	0.00	0.02	0.29	0.77
Bt-LN-Pesticide Cost	–0.08	0.06	–1.37	0.18
Bt-LN-Irrigation Charges	0.06	0.12	0.49	0.63
Bt-LN-Mechanization Cost	–0.19	0.17	–1.10	0.28
Bt-LN-Labour Cost	–0.10	0.13	–0.82	0.41

Yavatmal

Regression Statistics	
Multiple R	0.42
R Square	0.18
Adjusted R Square	0.04
Standard Error	0.29
Observations	70

	Coefficients	*Standard Error*	*t Stat*	*P-value*
Intercept	8.97	2.34	3.84	0.00
LN-NCA	0.14	0.10	1.49	0.14
Bt-LN-Seed Cost	0.04	0.33	0.12	0.90
Bt-LN-Fertilizer Cost	0.05	0.13	0.42	0.67
Bt-LN-Cost of Growth Regulators	0.01	0.02	0.62	0.54
Bt-LN-Cost of FVM	0.02	0.02	1.06	0.29
Bt-LN-Cost of Micronutrient	0.01	0.02	0.56	0.58
Bt-LN-Pesticide Cost	–0.06	0.07	–0.79	0.43
Bt-LN-Irrigation Charges	0.15	0.16	0.94	0.35
Bt-LN-Mechanization Cost	0.09	0.12	0.75	0.45
Bt-LN-Labour Cost	–0.09	0.11	–0.80	0.43

Southern Region

Andhra Pradesh

Adilabad

Regression Statistics	
Multiple R	0.38
R Square	0.14
Adjusted R Square	0.03
Standard Error	0.23
Observations	70

	Coefficients	*Standard Error*	*t Stat*	*P-value*
Intercept	9.34	1.32	7.06	0.00
LN-NCA.	0.06	0.06	1.01	0.32
Bt-LN-Seed Cost	–0.16	0.11	–1.42	0.16
Bt-LN-Fertilizer Cost	–0.11	0.12	–0.92	0.36
Bt-LN-Cost of Micronutrient	0.00	0.02	0.23	0.82
Bt-LN-Pesticide Cost	0.21	0.10	2.15	0.04
Bt-LN-Irrigation Charges	–0.02	0.10	–0.22	0.83
Bt-LN-Mechanization Cost	0.11	0.11	1.03	0.31
Bt-LN-Labour Cost	0.07	0.06	1.15	0.25

Warangal

Regression Statistics	
Multiple R	0.49
R Square	0.24
Adjusted R Square	0.11
Standard Error	0.27
Observations	70

	Coefficients	*Standard Error*	*t Stat*	*P-value*
Intercept	10.07	1.91	5.28	0.00
LN-NCA	0.16	0.06	2.87	0.01
Bt-LN-Seed Cost	0.15	0.14	1.02	0.31
Bt-LN-Fertilizer Cost	–0.13	0.16	–0.79	0.43
Bt-LN-Cost of Growth Regulators	0.02	0.02	1.11	0.27
Bt-UN-Cost of FYM	0.03	0.01	2.17	0.03
Bt-LN-Cost of Micronutrient	–0.01	0.01	–0.50	0.62
Bt-LN-Pesticide Cost	0.02	0.07	0.36	0.72
Bt-LN-Irrigation Charges	0.22	0.10	2.19	0.03
Bt-LN-Mechanization Cost	–0.11	0.10	–1.11	0.27
Bt-LN-Labour Cost	–0.02	0.09	–0.23	0.82

Karnataka

Dharwad

Regression Statistics	
Multiple R	0.42
R Square	0.18
Adjusted R Square	0.06
Standard Error	0.43
Observations	70

	Coefficients	*Standard Error*	*t Stat*	*P-value*
Intercept	11.97	2.09	5.73	0.00
LN-NCA	0.11	0.07	1.46	0.15
Bt-LN-Seed Cost	–0.04	0.14	–0.31	0.76
Bt-LN-Fertilizer Cost	–0.04	0.14	–0.31	0.76
Bt-LN-Cost of FYM	0.03	0.02	2.01	**0.05**
Bt-LN-Cost of Micronutrient	–0.04	0.04	–0.99	0.33
Bt-LN-Pesticide Cost	–0.10	0.09	–1.13	0.26
Bt-LN-Irrigation Charges	–0.18	0.18	–0.98	0.33
Bt-LN-Mechanization Cost	0.07	0.24	0.29	0.77
Bt-LN-Labour Cost	–0.01	0.11	–0.09	0.33

Tamil Nadu

Virudunagar

Regression Statistics	
Multiple R	0.49
R Square	0.24
Adjusted R Square	0.14
Standard Error	0.14
Observations	70

	Coefficients	*Standard Error*	*t Stat*	*P-value*
Intercept	12.43	1.54	8.05	0.00
LN-NCA	0.11	0.07	1.59	0.12
Bt-LN-Seed Cost	0.15	0.08	1.90	**0.06**
Bt-LN-Fertilizer Cost	0.03	0.05	0.67	0.51
Bt-LN-Cost of FYM	0.02	0.02	0.85	0.40
Bt–LN-Pesticide Cost	–0.08	0.04	–1.77	**0.08**
Bt-LN-Irrigation Charges	–0.06	0.04	–1.37	0.17
Bt-LN-Mechanization Cost	–0.41	0.15	–2.81	**0.01**
Bt-LN-Labour Cost	0.05	0.08	0.59	0.56

6

Farmers' Perception on the Impact of Bt Cotton on Income, Health and Livelihood Status

This chapter mainly deals with the perception of farmers in the cotton belt of India about the impact of cultivation of Bt cotton on yields, returns, seed usage and expenditure, pesticide usage and expenditure, pest attacks, irrigation expenditure, suicides, human health, livestock health, soil quality, as well as any perceptible impact on the environment. Apart from these, this chapter will also document the perception of farmers regarding issues of labour, credit and influence of weather on Bt cotton yields.

As regards yields and returns from Bt cotton *vis-à-vis* Non- Bt cotton is concerned, 95 per cent farmers said that Bt cotton yields were higher than Non-Bt cotton and 88 per cent said that returns were also higher. The proportions are very similar across all the surveyed districts and across different farm size categories (Table 6.1).

Perception on Yields and Returns

Table 6.1: Yields and Returns from Bt cotton *vis-à-vis* Non-Bt Cotton (%)

Regions	*States*	*Districts*	*Farm Size Categories*	*Yields of Bt-Cotton compared to Non-Bt Cotton*		*Returns from Bt-Cotton compared to Non-Bt cotton*	
				Higher	*Lesser*	*Higher*	*Lesser*
Northern Region	**Punjab**	**Bathinda**	Small	100	0	95	5
			Medium	96	4	100	0
			Large	100	0	100	0
			District Average	**98**	**2**	**99**	**1**

(Contd.)

Table 6.1 (*Contd.*)

Regions	*States*	*Districts*	*Farm Size Categories*	*Yields of Bt-Cotton compared to Non-Bt Cotton*		*Returns from Bt-Cotton compared to Non-Bt cotton*	
				Higher	*Lesser*	*Higher*	*Lesser*
		Fazilka	Small	100	0	100	0
			Medium	100	0	100	0
			Large	100	0	100	0
			District Average	**100**	**0**	**100**	**0**
		Punjab Average		**99**	**1**	**99**	**1**
	Haryana	**Hissar**	Small	96	4	88	12
			Medium	97	3	97	3
			Large	100	0	100	0
			District Average	**97**	**3**	**94**	**6**
		Sirsa	Small	95	5	100	0
			Medium	100	0	100	0
			Large	100	0	100	0
			District Average	**97**	**3**	**100**	**0**
		Haryana Average		**97**	**3**	**97**	**3**
	Rajasthan	**Hanumangarh**	Small	78	22	67	33
			Medium	100	0	100	0
			Large	100	0	100	0
			District Average	**89**	**11**	**83**	**17**
		Rajasthan Average		**89**	**11**	**83**	**17**
Central Region	**Gujarat**	**Bhavnagar**	Small	83	17	97	3
			Medium	76	24	95	5
			Large	50	50	100	0
			District Average	**77**	**23**	**97**	**3**
		Surendranagar	Small	90	10	90	10
			Medium	90	10	100	0
			Large	50	50	100	0
			District Average	**89**	**11**	**93**	**7**
		Gujarat Average		**83**	**17**	**94**	**6**
	Madhya Pradesh	**Dhar**	Small	100	0	95	5
			Medium	100	0	97	3
			Large	100	0	95	5
			District Average	**100**	**0**	**96**	**4**
		Khargone	Small	100	0	96	4
			Medium	100	0	100	0
			Large	100	0	93	7
			District Average	**100**	**0**	**97**	**3**
		Madhya Pradesh Average		**100**	**0**	**96**	**4**

(*Contd.*)

Table 6.1 (*Contd.*)

Regions	*States*	*Districts*	*Farm Size Categories*	*Yields of Bt-Cotton compared to Non-Bt Cotton*		*Returns from Bt-Cotton compared to Non-Bt cotton*	
				Higher	*Lesser*	*Higher*	*Lesser*
	Maharashtra	**Jalgaon**	Small	100	0	89	11
			Medium	100	0	94	6
			Large	100	0	100	0
			District Average	**100**	**0**	**93**	**7**
		Yavatmal	Small	100	0	78	22
			Medium	100	0	87	13
			Large	100	0	80	20
			District Average	**100**	**0**	**80**	**20**
		Maharashtra Average		**100**	**0**	**86**	**14**
Southern Region	**Andhra Pradesh**	**Adilabad**	Small	84	16	100	0
			Medium	87	13	100	0
			Large	100	0	100	0
			District Average	**90**	**10**	**100**	**0**
		Warangal	Small	93	7	85	15
			Medium	92	8	92	8
			Large	100	0	100	0
			District Average	**94**	**6**	**91**	**9**
		Andhra Pradesh Average		**91**	**9**	**94**	**6**
	Karnataka	**Dharwad**	Small	87	13	90	10
			Medium	100	0	95	5
			Large	100	0	100	0
			District Average	**91**	**9**	**93**	**7**
		Karnataka Average		**91**	**9**	**93**	**7**
	Tamil Nadu	**Virudunagar**	Small	98	2	0	100
			Medium	100	0	0	100
			Large	—	—	—	—
			District Average	**99**	**1**	**0**	**100**
		Tamil Nadu Average		**99**	**1**	**0**	**100**
ALL INDIA			Small	94	6	85	15
			Medium	96	4	90	10
			Large	93	7	98	2
			All India Average	**95**	**5**	**88**	**12**

Source: Primary Field Survey.

Knowledge of Bt Cotton

It would be seen from Table 6.2 that farmers knew of Bt cotton mainly from co-farmers (70%) followed by seed dealers (23%), extension workers (3%) and social media (4%). However, an exception was seen in case of Rajasthan and Maharashtra, where seed dealers provided most information on Bt cotton.

Table 6.2: Knowledge of Bt Cotton (%)

Regions	States	Districts	Farm Size Categories	Co-Farmers	Extension Workers	Seed Dealers	Media (TV, Radio, Newspapers)
Northern Region	**Punjab**	**Bathinda**	Small	90	0	10	0
			Medium	89	2	9	0
			Large	80	20	0	0
			District Average	**86**	**7**	**7**	**0**
		Fazilka	Small	90	0	10	0
			Medium	84	0	16	0
			Large	40	0	60	0
			District Average	**75**	**0**	**25**	**0**
		Punjab Average		**82**	**3**	**15**	**0**
	Haryana	**Hissar**	Small	83	0	13	4
			Medium	62	9	29	0
			Large	75	0	25	0
			District Average	**72**	**4**	**23**	**1**
		Sirsa	Small	97	0	3	0
			Medium	95	0	5	0
			Large	60	10	30	0
			District Average	**91**	**2**	**7**	**0**
		Haryana Average		**81**	**3**	**15**	**1**
	Rajasthan	**Hanumangarh**	Small	22	0	67	11
			Medium	44	0	56	0
			Large	0	0	100	0
			District Average	**26**	**0**	**70**	**4**
		Rajasthan Average		**26**	**0**	**70**	**4**
Central Region	**Gujarat**	**Bhavnagar**	Small	73	10	14	3
			Medium	51	11	24	14
			Large	25	25	25	25
			District Average	**59**	**11**	**20**	**10**
		Surendranagar	Small	83	2	2	13
			Medium	75	15	5	5
			Large	100	0	0	0
			District Average	**81**	**6**	**3**	**10**
		Gujarat Average		**70**	**9**	**11**	**10**
	Madhya Pradesh	**Dhar**	Small	95	5	0	0
			Medium	100	0	0	0
			Large	84	11	5	0
			District Average	**94**	**4**	**2**	**0**
		Khargone	Small	100	0	0	0
			Medium	88	3	9	0
			Large	93	0	0	7
			District Average	**94**	**1**	**4**	**1**
		Madhya Pradesh Average		**94**	**2**	**3**	**1**

(Contd.)

Table 6.2(*Contd.*)

Regions	*States*	*Districts*	*Farm Size Categories*	*Co-Farmers*	*Extension Workers*	*Seed Dealers*	*Media (TV, Radio, Newspapers)*
	Maharashtra	**Jalgaon**	Small	22	0	78	0
			Medium	6	6	88	0
			Large	0	0	100	0
			District Average	**16**	**1**	**83**	**0**
		Yavatmal	Small	22	2	76	0
			Medium	14	13	73	0
			Large	20	0	80	0
			District Average	**20**	**4**	**76**	**0**
		Maharashtra Average		**18**	**3**	**79**	**0**
Southern Region	**Andhra Pradesh**	**Adilabad**	Small	94	0	3	3
			Medium	61	10	6	23
			Large	100	0	0	0
			District Average	**81**	**4**	**4**	**11**
		Warangal	Small	93	0	0	7
			Medium	62	0	15	23
			Large	0	0	50	50
			District Average	**60**	**0**	**18**	**22**
		Andhra Pradesh Average		**78**	**2**	**7**	**13**
	Karnataka	**Dharwad**	Small	94	2	4	0
			Medium	74	0	26	0
			Large	100	0	0	0
			District Average	**89**	**1**	**10**	**0**
		Karnataka Average		**89**	**1**	**10**	**0**
	Tamil Nadu	**Virudunagar**	Small	100	0	0	0
			Medium	100	0	0	0
			Large	—	—	—	—
			District Average	**100**	**0**	**0**	**0**
		Tamil Nadu Average		**100**	**0**	**0**	**0**
ALL INDIA			Small	77	1	19	3
			Medium	67	5	24	4
			Large	56	5	34	6
			All India Average	**70**	**3**	**23**	**4**

Source: Primary Field Survey.

Perception of Seed Usage

Table 6.3 shows that 85 per cent farmers said that the quantity of seed usage per hectare in Bt cotton is less than that used in Non-Bt cotton. However, 93 per cent farmers said that the expenditure on Bt cotton seeds is more than Non-Bt cotton. The proportions are very similar across all the surveyed districts across different farm size categories.

Seed Usage

Table 6.3: Impact on Seed Usage on Bt Cotton *vis-à-vis* Non-Bt Cotton (%)

Regions	*States*	*Districts*	*Farm Size Categories*	*Seed usage per hectare in Bt-Cotton compared to Non-Bt Cotton*		*Expenditure on seed in Bt-Cotton compared to Non-Bt Cotton*	
				More	*Less*	*More*	*Less*
Northern Region	**Punjab**	**Bathinda**	Small	0	100	100	0
			Medium	2	98	100	0
			Large	0	100	100	0
			District Average	**1**	**99**	**100**	**0**
		Fazilka	Small	0	100	100	0
			Medium	0	100	100	0
			Large	0	100	100	0
			District Average	**0**	**100**	**100**	**0**
		Punjab Average		**1**	**99**	**100**	**0**
	Haryana	**Hissar**	Small	33	67	96	4
			Medium	24	76	97	3
			Large	25	75	100	0
			District Average	**27**	**73**	**98**	**2**
		Sirsa	Small	0	100	100	0
			Medium	0	100	95	5
			Large	0	100	100	0
			District Average	**0**	**100**	**98**	**2**
		Haryana Average		**15**	**85**	**98**	**2**
	Rajasthan	**Hanumangarh**	Small	0	100	98	2
			Medium	24	76	100	0
			Large	33	67	100	0
			District Average	**19**	**81**	**99**	**1**
		Rajasthan Average		**19**	**81**	**99**	**1**
Central Region	**Gujarat**	**Bhavnagar**	Small	7	93	97	3
			Medium	5	95	95	5
			Large	0	100	100	0
			District Average	**4**	**96**	**97**	**3**
		Surendranagar	Small	10	90	90	10
			Medium	5	95	90	10
			Large	0	100	100	0
			District Average	**6**	**94**	**93**	**7**
		Gujarat Average		**5**	**95**	**95**	**5**
	Madhya Pradesh	**Dhar**	Small	0	100	90	10
			Medium	0	100	97	3
			Large	0	100	100	0
			District Average	**0**	**100**	**96**	**4**
		Khargone	Small	9	91	100	0
			Medium	16	84	94	6
			Large	7	93	100	0
			District Average	**11**	**89**	**98**	**2**
		Madhya Pradesh Average		**6**	**94**	**97**	**3**
	Maharashtra	**Jalgaon**	Small	47	53	70	30
			Medium	22	78	82	18
			Large	29	71	100	0
			District Average	**35**	**65**	**84**	**16**

(*Contd.*)

Table 6.3 (*Contd.*)

Regions	*States*	*Districts*	*Farm Size Categories*	*Seed usage per hectare in Bt-Cotton compared to Non-Bt Cotton*		*Expenditure on seed in Bt-Cotton compared to Non-Bt Cotton*	
				More	*Less*	*More*	*Less*
		Yavatmal	Small	48	52	70	30
			Medium	47	53	100	0
			Large	0	100	80	20
			District Average	**32**	**68**	**83**	**17**
		Maharashtra Average		**33**	**67**	**83**	**17**
Southern Region	**Andhra Pradesh**	**Adilabad**	Small	32	68	70	30
			Medium	29	71	74	26
			Large	50	50	100	0
			District Average	**35**	**65**	**81**	**19**
		Warangal	Small	4	96	100	0
			Medium	15	85	100	0
			Large	0	100	100	0
			District Average	**6**	**94**	**100**	**0**
		Andhra Pradesh Average		**20**	**80**	**91**	**9**
	Karnataka	**Dharwad**	Small	23	77	75	25
			Medium	32	68	83	17
			Large	33	67	67	33
			District Average	**26**	**74**	**75**	**25**
		Karnataka Average		**26**	**74**	**75**	**25**
	Tamil Nadu	**Virudunagar**	Small	42	58	82	18
			Medium	20	80	90	10
			Large	—	—	—	—
			District Average	**36**	**64**	**84**	**16**
		Tamil Nadu Average		**36**	**64**	**84**	**16**
ALL INDIA			Small	17	83	89	11
			Medium	16	84	93	7
			Large	13	87	96	4
			All India Average	**15**	**85**	**93**	**7**

Source: Primary Field Survey.

Perception on Spurious Seeds

Small proportion of farmers (4%) said that they had faced problems of spurious seeds. Most of the States conformed to this, excepting Gujarat, wherein 21 per cent farmers said that they had faced such a problem. Otherwise, the proportions are very similar across all the surveyed districts across different farm size categories (Table 6.4).

Table 6.4: Proportion of Farmers who faced Problems of Spurious Seeds (%)

Regions	*States*	*Districts*	*Farm Size Categories*	*Yes*	*No*
Northern Region	**Punjab**	**Bathinda**	Small	0	100
			Medium	0	100
			Large	0	100
			District Average	**0**	**100**
		Fazilka	Small	0	100
			Medium	0	100
			Large	0	100
			District Average	**0**	**100**
		Punjab Average		**0**	**100**
	Haryana	**Hissar**	Small	8	92
			Medium	6	94
			Large	0	100
			District Average	**5**	**95**
		Sirsa	Small	0	100
			Medium	0	100
			Large	0	100
			District Average	**0**	**100**
		Haryana Average		**3**	**97**
	Rajasthan	**Hanumangarh**	Small	0	100
			Medium	0	100
			Large	0	100
			District Average	**0**	**100**
		Rajasthan Average		**0**	**100**
Central Region	**Gujarat**	**Bhavnagar**	Small	10	90
			Medium	11	89
			Large	50	50
			District Average	**24**	**76**
		Surendranagar	Small	4	96
			Medium	0	100
			Large	50	50
			District Average	**18**	**82**
		Gujarat Average		**21**	**79**
	Madhya Pradesh	**Dhar**	Small	0	100
			Medium	0	100
			Large	0	100
			District Average	**0**	**100**
		Khargone	Small	0	100
			Medium	0	100
			Large	0	100
			District Average	**0**	**100**
		Madhya Pradesh Average		**0**	**100**
	Maharashtra	**Jalgaon**	Small	0	100
			Medium	0	100
			Large	0	100
			District Average	0	100

(Contd.)

Table 6.4 *(Contd.)*

Regions	*States*	*Districts*	*Farm Size Categories*	*Yes*	*No*
		Yavatmal	Small	2	98
			Medium	0	100
			Large	0	100
			District Average	**1**	**99**
		Maharashtra Average		**1**	**99**
Southern Region	**Andhra Pradesh**	**Adilabad**	Small	0	100
			Medium	10	90
			Large	0	100
			District Average	**3**	**97**
		Warangal	Small	4	96
			Medium	15	85
			Large	0	100
			District Average	**6**	**94**
		Andhra Pradesh Average		**5**	**95**
	Karnataka	**Dharwad**	Small	0	100
			Medium	5	95
			Large	0	100
			District Average	**1**	**99**
		Karnataka Average		**1**	**99**
	Tamil Nadu	**Virudunagar**	Small	0	100
			Medium	5	95
			Large	—	—
			District Average	**2**	**98**
		Tamil Nadu Average		**2**	**98**
ALL INDIA			Small	2	98
			Medium	3	97
			Large	7	93
			All India Average	**4**	**96**

Source: Primary Field Survey.

Perception on 'Refugia'

To get better yields, it is emphasized that cotton farmers should plant a 'Refugia' of Non-Bt cotton crop along with Bt cotton to maintain the effectiveness of Bt cotton seeds. However, from Table 6.5, it is seen that 85 per cent of the farmers did not plant the refuge crops alongside their Bt cotton plots. This is because farmers look at getting higher yields and earn higher income on maximum areas, which are just short-term gains. Further, the proportions are generally skewed towards large farmers in most of thc surveyed districts. This means that small farmers are taking more risk by devoting the entire area to Bt cotton in order to derive maximum benefits.

Table 6.5: Proportion of Farmers Cultivating Refuge Crops

Regions	*States*	*Districts*	*Farm Size Categories*	*'Refuge'*	
				Planted	*Not Planted*
Northern Region	**Punjab**	**Bathinda**	Small	20	80
			Medium	13	87
			Large	40	60
			District Average	**20**	**80**
		Fazilka	Small	0	100
			Medium	0	100
			Large	0	100
			District Average	**0**	**100**
		Punjab Average		**10**	**90**
	Haryana	**Hissar**	Small	17	83
			Medium	24	76
			Large	33	67
			District Average	**23**	**77**
		Sirsa	Small	13	87
			Medium	32	68
			Large	30	70
			District Average	**24**	**76**
		Haryana Average		**24**	**77**
	Rajasthan	**Hanumangarh**	Small	11	89
			Medium	16	84
			Large	33	67
			District Average	**18**	**82**
		Rajasthan Average		**18**	**82**
Central Region	**Gujarat**	**Bhavnagar**	Small	17	83
			Medium	24	76
			Large	25	75
			District Average	**21**	**79**
		Surendranagar	Small	21	79
			Medium	25	75
			Large	50	50
			District Average	**28**	**72**
		Gujarat Average		**24**	**76**
	Madhya Pradesh	**Dhar**	Small	0	100
			Medium	7	93
			Large	21	79
			District Average	**9**	**91**
		Khargone	Small	0	100
			Medium	13	87
			Large	33	67
			District Average	**14**	**86**
		Madhya Pradesh Average		**11**	**89**
	Maharashtra	**Jalgaon**	Small	2	98
			Medium	11	89
			Large	29	71
			District Average	**11**	**89**
		Yavatmal	Small	4	96
			Medium	0	100
			Large	40	60
			District Average	**14**	**86**
		Maharashtra Average		**13**	**87**

(Contd.)

Table 6.5 (*Contd.*)

Regions	*States*	*Districts*	*Farm Size Categories*	*'Refuge'*	
				Planted	*Not Planted*
Southern Region	**Andhra Pradesh**	**Adilabad**	Small	11	89
			Medium	6	94
			Large	0	100
			District Average	**7**	**93**
		Warangal	Small	18	82
			Medium	15	85
			Large	0	100
			District Average	**12**	**88**
		Andhra Pradesh Average		**10**	**90**
	Karnataka	**Dharwad**	Small	8	92
			Medium	11	89
			Large	67	33
			District Average	**25**	**75**
		Karnataka Average		**25**	**75**
	Tamil Nadu	**Virudunagar**	Small	10	90
			Medium	20	80
			Large	—	—
			District Average	**13**	**87**
		Tamil Nadu Average		**13**	**87**
ALL INDIA			Small	10	90
			Medium	14	86
			Large	29	71
			All India Average	**15**	**85**

Source: Primary Field Survey.

Perception on Fertilizer Use

As regards fertilizer consumption (Table 6.6), the total fertilizer usage on Bt cotton was reported to be slightly higher (54%) than Non-Bt cotton (46%). In the northern States of Punjab, Haryana and Rajasthan, large proportion of farmers reported higher usage of fertilizer on Bt cotton. The proportions are 100 per cent in Rajasthan, 96 per cent in Punjab and 85 per cent in Haryana. In some of the central and southern States, interestingly, fertilizer usage has been reported to be higher in case on Non-Bt cotton compared to Bt cotton. In Gujarat, 85 per cent farmers reported high usage of fertilizers on Non-Bt cotton. The proportions are 95 per cent for Madhya Pradesh, 52 per cent for Karnataka, 99 per cent for Tamil Nadu. The States of Maharashtra and Andhra Pradesh present a mixed picture. In the Yavatmal district of Maharashtra 100 per cent farmers reported higher usage of fertilizers on Bt cotton, whereas in the Jalgaon district 28 per cent farmers reported higher usage of fertilizers on Non-Bt cotton. Overall, in Maharashtra, 72 per cent farmers reported higher usage of fertilizers on Bt cotton compared to Non-Bt cotton. Similarly, in the

Warangal district of Andhra Pradesh 94 per cent farmers reported higher usage of fertilizers on Bt cotton, whereas in the Adilabad district 70 per cent farmers reported higher usage of fertilizers on Non-Bt cotton. Overall, in Andhra Pradesh, 64 per cent farmers reported higher usage of fertilizers on Bt cotton compared to Non-Bt cotton.

Table 6.6: Fertilizer Usage on Bt Cotton *vis-à-vis* Non-Bt Cotton (%)

Regions	*States*	*Districts*	*Farm Size Categories*	*More Fertilizer*	*Less Fertilizer*
Northern Region	**Punjab**	**Bathinda**	Small	100	0
			Medium	96	4
			Large	100	0
			District Average	**99**	**1**
		Fazilka	Small	80	20
			Medium	100	0
			Large	100	0
			District Average	**93**	**7**
		Punjab Average		**96**	**4**
	Haryana	**Hissar**	Small	62	38
			Medium	76	24
			Large	92	8
			District Average	**74**	**26**
		Sirsa	Small	92	8
			Medium	100	0
			Large	100	0
			District Average	**96**	**4**
		Haryana Average		**85**	**15**
	Rajasthan	**Hanumangarh**	Small	100	0
			Medium	100	0
			Large	100	0
			District Average	**100**	**0**
		Rajasthan Average		**100**	**0**
Central Region	**Gujarat**	**Bhavnagar**	Small	10	90
			Medium	8	92
			Large	0	100
			District Average	**7**	**93**
		Surendranagar	Small	6	94
			Medium	5	95
			Large	50	50
			District Average	**20**	**80**
		Gujarat Average		**13**	**87**
	Madhya Pradesh	**Dhar**	Small	14	86
			Medium	20	80
			Large	0	100
			District Average	**11**	**89**
		Khargone	Small	4	96
			Medium	9	91
			Large	0	100
			District Average	**5**	**95**
		Madhya Pradesh Average		**9**	**91**

(Contd.)

Table 6.6 (*Contd.*)

Regions	*States*	*Districts*	*Farm Size Categories*	*More Fertilizer*	*Less Fertilizer*
	Maharashtra	**Jalgaon**	Small	60	40
			Medium	17	83
			Large	0	100
			District Average	**28**	**72**
		Yavatmal	Small	100	0
			Medium	100	0
			Large	100	0
			District Average	**100**	**0**
		Maharashtra Average		**70**	**30**
Southern Region	**Andhra Pradesh**	**Adilabad**	Small	27	73
			Medium	52	48
			Large	0	100
			District Average	**30**	**70**
		Warangal	Small	96	4
			Medium	85	15
			Large	100	0
			District Average	**94**	**6**
		Andhra Pradesh Average		**64**	**36**
	Karnataka	**Dharwad**	Small	40	60
			Medium	42	58
			Large	67	33
			District Average	**48**	**52**
		Karnataka Average		**48**	**52**
	Tamil Nadu	**Virudunagar**	Small	2	98
			Medium	0	100
			Large	—	—
			District Average	**1**	**99**
		Tamil Nadu Average		**1**	**99**
ALL INDIA			Small	53	47
			Medium	54	46
			Large	58	42
			All India Average	**54**	**46**

Source: Primary Field Survey.

Perception on Pesticide Use

At the all India level, 77 per cent farmers reported that the quantity of pesticide usage on Bt cotton had reduced over the years, while 79 per cent said that the expenditure on pesticide use for Bt cotton had also reduced (Table 6.7). However, a relatively higher proportion of farmers (63%) in the Hanumangarh district of Rajasthan, Yavatmal district of Maharashtra (90%) and Virudunagar district of Tamil Nadu (79%) reported an increase in pesticide usage and a commensurate increase in pesticide expenditure.

Table 6.7: Quantity and Expenditure on Pesticide Usage on Bt Cotton (%)

Regions	*States*	*Districts*	*Farm Size Categories*	*Quantity of Pesticides Used*		*Expenditure on Pesticides*	
				Reduced	*Increased*	*Reduced*	*Increased*
Northern Region	**Punjab**	**Bathinda**	Small	95	5	95	5
			Medium	87	13	73	27
			Large	100	0	100	0
			District Average	**93**	**7**	**88**	**12**
		Fazilka	Small	87	13	100	0
			Medium	100	0	100	0
			Large	100	0	100	0
			District Average	**95**	**5**	**100**	**0**
		Punjab Average		**94**	**6**	**92**	**8**
	Haryana	**Hissar**	Small	79	21	75	25
			Medium	88	12	85	15
			Large	100	0	100	0
			District Average	**87**	**13**	**86**	**14**
		Sirsa	Small	89	11	66	34
			Medium	91	9	77	23
			Large	70	30	80	20
			District Average	**87**	**13**	**71**	**29**
		Haryana Average		**87**	**13**	**78**	**22**
	Rajasthan	**Hanumangarh**	Small	44	56	56	44
			Medium	28	72	60	40
			Large	33	67	33	67
			District Average	**37**	**63**	**54**	**46**
		Rajasthan Average		**37**	**63**	**54**	**46**
Central Region	**Gujarat**	**Bhavnagar**	Small	90	10	86	14
			Medium	89	11	95	5
			Large	75	25	75	25
			District Average	**89**	**11**	**90**	**10**
		Surendranagar	Small	92	8	98	2
			Medium	95	5	100	0
			Large	100	0	100	0
			District Average	**94**	**6**	**99**	**1**
		Gujarat Average		**91**	**9**	**94**	**6**
	Madhya Pradesh	**Dhar**	Small	100	0	100	0
			Medium	100	0	100	0
			Large	100	0	100	0
			District Average	**100**	**0**	**100**	**0**
		Khargone	Small	100	0	100	0
			Medium	97	3	100	0
			Large	100	0	100	0
			District Average	**99**	**1**	**100**	**0**
		Madhya Pradesh Average		**99**	**1**	**100**	**0**
	Maharashtra	**Jalgaon**	Small	62	38	64	36
			Medium	83	17	83	17
			Large	100	0	100	0
			District Average	**80**	**20**	**89**	**20**
		Yavatmal	Small	24	76	34	66
			Medium	0	100	0	100
			Large	0	100	20	80
			District Average	**10**	**90**	**20**	**80**
		Maharashtra Average		**44**	**56**	**55**	**45**

(Contd.)

Table 6.7 (*Contd.*)

Regions	*States*	*Districts*	*Farm Size Categories*	*Quantity of Pesticides Used*		*Expenditure on Pesticides*	
				Reduced	*Increased*	*Reduced*	*Increased*
Southern Region	**Andhra Pradesh**	**Adilabad**	Small	100	0	100	
			Medium	100	0	100	0
			Large	100	0	100	0
			District Average	**100**	**0**	**100**	**0**
		Warangal	Small	95	5	91	9
			Medium	92	8	92	8
			Large	100	0	100	0
			District Average	**94**	**6**	**93**	**7**
		Andhra Pradesh Average		**97**	**3**	**96**	**4**
	Karnataka	**Dharwad**	Small	54	46	65	35
			Medium	79	21	47	53
			Large	100	0	100	0
			District Average	**75**	**25**	**69**	**31**
		Karnataka Average		**75**	**25**	**69**	**31**
	Tamil Nadu	**Virudunagar**	Small	16	84	30	70
			Medium	35	65	50	50
			Large	—	—	—	—
			District Average	**21**	**79**	**36**	**64**
		Tamil Nadu Average		**21**	**79**	**36**	**64**
ALL INDIA			Small	75	25	77	23
			Medium	78	22	77	23
			Large	84	16	85	15
			All India Average	**77**	**23**	**79**	**21**

Source: Primary Field Survey.

Perception on Bollworm Attack

As regards the role of Bt cotton in minimizing the attack of Bollworm (Table 6.8), it is seen that at the all India level, 90 per cent farmers claimed that Bt cotton had reduced the attack of Bollworms. Across the States and districts the proportion of farmers claiming the reduction of Bollworm attack was similar, i.e., around the all India average of 90 per cent. The proportions are very similar across all the surveyed districts across different farm size categories. Only in certain regions like Sirsa, Dharwad and Virudunagar, relatively higher proportion of farmers (30-40%) reported that the attacks of Bollworm had increased. Farmers said that with the introduction of Bt cotton, though Bollworm damage had declined, there was an increased damage of sucking pests such as Jassids, White flies, Thrips, and Mealy bugs as well as bacterial, fungal and viral diseases. As a consequence insecticide usage was increasing gradually in certain areas.

Table 6.8: Role of Bt Cotton in Minimising Bollworm Attack (%)

Regions	*States*	*Districts*	*Farm Size Categories*	*Yes*	*No*
Northern Region	**Punjab**	**Bathinda**	Small	100	0
			Medium	100	0
			Large	100	0
			District Average	**100**	**0**
		Fazilka	Small	100	0
			Medium	100	0
			Large	100	0
			District Average	**100**	**0**
		Punjab Average		**100**	**0**
	Haryana	**Hissar**	Small	92	8
			Medium	85	15
			Large	100	0
			District Average	**91**	**9**
		Sirsa	Small	74	26
			Medium	77	23
			Large	40	60
			District Average	**67**	**33**
		Haryana Average		**79**	**21**
	Rajasthan	**Hanumangarh**	Small	78	22
			Medium	88	12
			Large	100	0
			District Average	**88**	**12**
		Rajasthan Average		**88**	**12**
Central Region	**Gujarat**	**Bhavnagar**	Small	86	14
			Medium	95	5
			Large	75	25
			District Average	**90**	**10**
		Surendranagar	Small	100	0
			Medium	100	0
			Large	100	0
			District Average	**100**	**0**
		Gujarat Average		**95**	**5**
	Madhya Pradesh	**Dhar**	Small	100	0
			Medium	100	0
			Large	100	0
			District Average	**100**	**0**
		Khargone	Small	100	0
			Medium	100	0
			Large	100	0
			District Average	**100**	**0**
		Madhya Pradesh Average		**100**	**0**
	Maharashtra	**Jalgaon**	Small	100	0
			Medium	100	0
			Large	100	0
			District Average	**100**	**0**
		Yavatmal	Small	98	2
			Medium	100	0
			Large	100	0
			District Average	**99**	**1**
		Maharashtra Average		**99**	**1**

(Contd.)

Table 6.8 (*Contd.*)

Regions	*States*	*Districts*	*Farm Size Categories*	*Yes*	*No*
Southern Region	**Andhra Pradesh**	**Adilabad**	Small	100	0
			Medium	100	0
			Large	100	0
			District Average	**100**	**0**
		Warangal	Small	93	7
			Medium	92	8
			Large	100	0
			District Average	**94**	**6**
		Andhra Pradesh Average		**96**	**4**
	Karnataka	**Dharwad**	Small	67	33
			Medium	79	21
			Large	67	33
			District Average	**70**	**30**
		Karnataka Average		**70**	**30**
	Tamil Nadu	**Virudunagar**	Small	52	48
			Medium	60	40
			Large	—	—
			District Average	**56**	**44**
		Tamil Nadu Average		**56**	**44**
ALL INDIA			Small	89	11
			Medium	92	8
			Large	90	10
			All India Average	**90**	**10**

Source: Primary Field Survey.

Perception on Irrigation Expenditure

As regards irrigation expenditure a relatively higher proportion of farmers (65%) said that irrigation expenditure on Bt cotton was higher than Non-Bt cotton (Table 6.9). In the surveyed States of Punjab, Haryana, Rajasthan, Maharashtra, Gujarat and Andhra Pradesh majority farmers reported higher expenditure on irrigation in Bt cotton compared to Non-Bt cotton. In the States of Madhya Pradesh and Tamil Nadu, relatively higher proportion of farmers reported higher expenditure for Non-Bt cotton compared to Bt cotton.

Table 6.9: Irrigation Expenditure on Bt Cotton *vis-à-vis* Non-Bt Cotton (%)

Regions	*States*	*Districts*	*Farm Size Categories*	*Higher*	*Lower*
Northern Region	**Punjab**	**Bathinda**	Small	65	35
			Medium	53	47
			Large	60	40
			District Average	**57**	**43**

(*Contd.*)

Table 6.9 (*Contd.*)

Regions	*States*	*Districts*	*Farm Size Categories*	*Higher*	*Lower*
		Fazilka	Small	100	0
			Medium	92	8
			Large	60	40
			District Average	**82**	**18**
		Punjab Average		**75**	**25**
	Haryana	**Hissar**	Small	79	21
			Medium	82	18
			Large	67	33
			District Average	**79**	**21**
		Sirsa	Small	95	5
			Medium	91	9
			Large	100	0
			District Average	**95**	**5**
		Haryana Average		**86**	**14**
	Rajasthan	**Hanumangarh**	Small	100	0
			Medium	100	0
			Large	100	0
			District Average	**100**	**0**
		Rajasthan Average		**100**	**0**
Central Region	**Gujarat**	**Bhavnagar**	Small	72	28
			Medium	68	32
			Large	100	0
			District Average	**80**	**20**
		Surendranagar	Small	73	27
			Medium	85	15
			Large	100	0
			District Average	**87**	**13**
		Gujarat Average		**83**	**17**
	Madhya Pradesh	**Dhar**	Small	38	62
			Medium	37	63
			Large	47	53
			District Average	**40**	**60**
		Khargone	Small	9	91
			Medium	25	75
			Large	13	87
			District Average	**17**	**83**
		Madhya Pradesh Average		**29**	**71**
	Maharashtra	**Jalgaon**	Small	67	33
			Medium	61	39
			Large	57	43
			District Average	**64**	**36**
		Yavatmal	Small	74	26
			Medium	80	20
			Large	80	20
			District Average	**76**	**24**
		Maharashtra Average		**70**	**30**
Southern Region	**Andhra Pradesh**	**Adilabad**	Small	43	57
			Medium	39	61
			Large	100	0
			District Average	**60**	**40**

(*Contd.*)

Table 6.9 (*Contd.*)

Regions	*States*	*Districts*	*Farm Size Categories*	*Higher*	*Lower*
		Warangal	Small	96	4
			Medium	92	8
			Large	100	0
			District Average	**96**	**4**
		Andhra Pradesh Average		**72**	**28**
	Karnataka	**Dharwad**	Small	52	48
			Medium	42	58
			Large	67	33
			District Average	**50**	**50**
		Karnataka Average		**50**	**50**
	Tamil Nadu	**Virudunagar**	Small	14	86
			Medium	5	95
			Large	0	0
			District Average	**11**	**89**
		Tamil Nadu Average		**11**	**89**
ALL INDIA			Small	65	35
			Medium	63	37
			Large	75	25
			All India Average	**65**	**35**

Source: Primary Field Survey.

Perception on Farmers' Suicides

As regards farmers' suicides, 5 per cent small farmers in Jalgaon and Yavatmal districts of Maharashtra and 3 per cent medium farmers in Adilabad district and 2 per cent small farmers in the Warangal district of Andhra Pradesh reported farm related suicide within their families (Table 6.10). Further, it needs to be mentioned that farmers in the central Indian region blamed the suicides on three major issues rather than the Bt cotton crop *per se*. These issues are as follows:

- Farmers of the central Indian regions said that the cotton crop is affected by vagaries of weather and that low rainfall affected Cotton crop yields. It is to be pointed out that around 90 per cent of Cotton area in the Central and Southern Indian regions are mainly rainfed (Chapter 4, Table 4.5). The insufficient water due to lack of irrigation results in lower yields. An important fact needs to be mentioned in connection with farm suicides, relatively low yields of Bt cotton in recent years and slight increase in pesticide consumption in certain regions. According to Blaise and Kranthi (2011), most of the Cotton grown in the country is rain-dependent and the crop experiences moisture stress. Furthermore, Cotton is grown on soils of varying depths, and it has been observed that productivity is better on deep vertisols (black soil) compared to the shallow soils because the former has a better water-holding capacity. Apart from productivity being affected, Cry toxin expression may also be affected. Water stress has been reported to affect expression of transgenes in transgenic crops such as Maize4, Peas5 and cotton. This has serious implications: (i) ineffective pest control; (ii) pest becoming resistant to the Bt toxin, and (iii) high pesticide use. Under rain-fed conditions of central India, rains cease early in September. Thus, the crops grown in deep vertisols are less likely to experience moisture stress than those grown on shallow soils. The study suggests that the Cry toxin concentration is affected by soil depth mainly due to the differences in soil water-holding capacity. Toxin concentration was optimal when the soils were close to field capacity. Soil moisture stress (excess as well as deficit) had an adverse effect on the toxin production.

- Farmers also complained about low and fluctuating Cotton prices over the years, which make the Cotton crop production risky and non-remunerative in some years.
- Lastly, farmers complained of unavailability of credit on time as a major concern. The huge transaction and borrowing costs associated with getting loans from institutional sources of credit was proving to be a cumbersome process for farmers especially for the small and medium farmers. Hence, these farmers depended more on non-institutional sources of credit such as money lenders, *arhatiyas* (middle men), relatives and friends wherein, on the one hand, transactions associated with getting loans was less cumbersome compared to getting loans from institutional sources, but on the other hand it was ridden with huge risks such as higher rates of interest and familial problems (Table 6.11). Thus, there is an imperative need for better institutional sources of credit that are high on efficiency and low on burdensome transaction costs.

Table 6.10: Proportion of Farm Households reporting Farmer Suicides (%)

Regions	*States*	*Districts*	*Farm Size Categories*	*Yes*	*No*
Northern Region	**Punjab**	**Bathinda**	Small	0	100
			Medium	0	100
			Large	0	100
			District Average	**0**	**100**
		Fazilka	Small	0	100
			Medium	0	100
			Large	0	100
			District Average	**0**	**100**
		Punjab Average		**0**	**100**

(Contd.)

Table 6.10 (*Contd.*)

Regions	*States*	*Districts*	*Farm Size Categories*	*Yes*	*No*
	Haryana	**Hissar**	Small	0	100
			Medium	0	100
			Large	0	100
			District Average	**0**	**100**
		Sirsa	Small	0	100
			Medium	0	100
			Large	0	100
			District Average	**0**	**100**
		Haryana Average		**0**	**100**
	Rajasthan	**Hanumangarh**	Small	0	100
			Medium	0	100
			Large	0	100
			District Average	**0**	**100**
		Rajasthan Average		**0**	**100**
Central Region	**Gujarat**	**Bhavnagar**	Small	0	100
			Medium	0	100
			Large	0	100
			District Average	**0**	**100**
		Surendranagar	Small	0	100
			Medium	0	100
			Large	0	100
			District Average	**0**	**100**
		Gujarat Average		**0**	**100**
	Madhya Pradesh	**Dhar**	Small	0	100
			Medium	0	100
			Large	0	100
			District Average	**0**	**100**
		Khargone	Small	0	100
			Medium	0	100
			Large	0	100
			District Average	**0**	**100**
		Madhya Pradesh Average		**0**	**100**
	Maharashtra	**Jalgaon**	Small	5	95
			Medium	0	100
			Large	0	100
			District Average	**3**	**97**
		Yavatmal	Small	5	95
			Medium	0	100
			Large	0	100
			District Average	**3**	**97**
		Maharashtra Average		**3**	**97**
Southern Region	**Andhra Pradesh**	**Adilabad**	Small	0	100
			Medium	3	97
			Large	0	100
			District Average	**1**	**99**
		Warangal	Small	2	98
			Medium	0	100
			Large	0	100
			District Average	**1**	**99**
		Andhra Pradesh Average		**1**	**99**

(*Contd.*)

Table 6.10 (*Contd.*)

Regions	States	Districts	Farm Size Categories	Yes	No
	Karnataka	**Dharwad**	Small	0	100
			Medium	0	100
			Large	0	100
			District Average	**0**	**100**
		Karnataka Average		**0**	**100**
	Tamil Nadu	**Virudunagar**	Small	0	100
			Medium	0	100
			Large	0	0
			District Average	**0**	**100**
		Tamil Nadu Average		**0**	**100**
ALL INDIA			Small	1	99
			Medium	0	100
			Large	0	100
			All India Average	**1**	**99**

Source: Primary Field Survey.

Perception on Credit

Table 6.11: Proportion of Farmers taking Credit from Institutional *vis-à-vis* Non-Institutional Sources

Regions	States	Districts	Farm Size Categories	Institutional Credit	Non-Institutional Credit
Northern Region	**Punjab**	**Bathinda**	Small	52	48
			Medium	15	85
			Large	40	60
			District Average	**26**	**74**
		Fazilka	Small	0	100
			Medium	0	100
			Large	0	100
			District Average	**0**	**100**
		Punjab Average		**16**	**84**
	Haryana	**Hissar**	Small	21	79
			Medium	44	56
			Large	80	20
			District Average	**44**	**56**
		Sirsa	Small	3	97
			Medium	40	60
			Large	30	70
			District Average	**19**	**81**
		Haryana Average		**32**	**68**
	Rajasthan	**Hanumangarh**	Small	29	71
			Medium	40	60
			Large	50	50
			District Average	**36**	**64**
		Rajasthan Average		**36**	**64**

(*Contd.*)

Table 6.11 (*Contd.*)

Regions	*States*	*Districts*	*Farm Size Categories*	*Institutional Credit*	*Non-Institutional Credit*
Central Region	**Gujarat**	**Bhavnagar**	Small	21	79
			Medium	30	70
			Large	0	100
			District Average	**19**	**81**
		Surendranagar	Small	29	71
			Medium	50	50
			Large	100	0
			District Average	**52**	**48**
		Gujarat Average		**31**	**69**
	Madhya Pradesh	**Dhar**	Small	38	62
			Medium	30	70
			Large	21	79
			District Average	**30**	**70**
		Khargone	Small	4	96
			Medium	13	88
			Large	0	100
			District Average	**7**	**93**
		Madhya Pradesh Average		**19**	**81**
	Maharashtra	**Jalgaon**	Small	9	91
			Medium	11	89
			Large	43	57
			District Average	**13**	**87**
		Yavatmal	Small	29	71
			Medium	29	71
			Large	29	71
			District Average	**29**	**71**
		Maharashtra Average		**23**	**77**
Southern Region	**Andhra Pradesh**	**Adilabad**	Small	13	87
			Medium	10	90
			Large	0	100
			District Average	**9**	**91**
		Warangal	Small	42	58
			Medium	47	53
			Large	50	50
			District Average	**43**	**57**
		Andhra Pradesh Average		**26**	**74**
	Karnataka	**Dharwad**	Small	33	67
			Medium	35	65
			Large	33	67
			District Average	**34**	**66**
		Karnataka Average		**34**	**66**
	Tamil Nadu	**Virudunagar**	Small	46	54
			Medium	40	60
			Large	—	—
			District Average	**44**	**56**
		Tamil Nadu Average		**44**	**56**
ALL INDIA			Small	25	75
			Medium	28	72
			Large	33	67
			All India Average	**27**	**73**

Source: Primary Field Survey.

Perception on Labour Use

At the all India level, 83 per cent farmers reported labour shortage problems (Table 6.12). In all the surveyed districts majority of the farmers reported such a problem. Among different size classes of farmers, mainly the large farmers reported the shortage of labour. The main reason assigned to the labour shortage problem was absorption of labour under the Mahatma Gandhi National Rural Employment Guarantee Act. With MNREGA providing 100 days of guaranteed work, timely availability of labourers especially during the Cotton picking season was a problem. Farmers said that labour costs had been increasing over the years due to shortage of labour. Table 7.3 (in Chapter 7) shows that daily wage rates of labourers in the Cotton cultivating regions were much higher than the national averages provided by the Ministry of Labour and Environment, GoI and also fixed slightly higher than the revised wage rate of MNREGA.

Table 6.12: Labour Shortage Problems (%)

Regions	*States*	*Districts*	*Farm Size Categories*	*Yes*	*No*
Northern Region	**Punjab**	**Bathinda**	Small	100	0
			Medium	100	0
			Large	100	0
			District Average	**100**	**0**
		Fazilka	Small	90	10
			Medium	16	84
			Large	0	100
			District Average	**45**	**55**
		Punjab Average		**71**	**29**
	Haryana	**Hissar**	Small	79	21
			Medium	91	9
			Large	92	8
			District Average	**87**	**13**
		Sirsa	Small	55	45
			Medium	64	36
			Large	60	40
			District Average	**59**	**41**
		Haryana Average		**73**	**27**
	Rajasthan	**Hanumangarh**	Small	67	33
			Medium	88	12
			Large	67	33
			District Average	**74**	**26**
		Rajasthan Average		**74**	**26**

(Contd.)

Table 6.12 (*Contd.*)

Regions	*States*	*Districts*	*Farm Size Categories*	*Yes*	*No*
Central Region	**Gujarat**	**Bhavnagar**	Small	62	38
			Medium	92	8
			Large	100	0
			District Average	**80**	**20**
		Surendranagar	Small	81	19
			Medium	85	15
			Large	100	0
			District Average	**83**	**17**
		Gujarat Average		**81**	**19**
	Madhya Pradesh	**Dhar**	Small	81	19
			Medium	83	17
			Large	79	21
			District Average	**81**	**19**
		Khargone	Small	91	9
			Medium	78	22
			Large	100	0
			District Average	**87**	**13**
		Madhya Pradesh Average		**84**	**16**
	Maharashtra	**Jalgaon**	Small	98	2
			Medium	94	6
			Large	100	0
			District Average	**97**	**3**
		Yavatmal	Small	98	2
			Medium	87	13
			Large	100	0
			District Average	**96**	**4**
		Maharashtra Average		**96**	**4**
Southern Region	**Andhra Pradesh**	**Adilabad**	Small	100	0
			Medium	94	6
			Large	100	0
			District Average	**97**	**3**
		Warangal	Small	87	13
			Medium	100	0
			Large	100	0
			District Average	**92**	**8**
		Andhra Pradesh Average		**94**	**6**
	Karnataka	**Dharwad**	Small	81	19
			Medium	79	21
			Large	67	33
			District Average	**80**	**20**
		Karnataka Average		**80**	**20**

(*Contd.*)

Table 6.12 (*Contd.*)

Regions	States	Districts	Farm Size Categories	Yes	No
	Tamil Nadu	**Virudunagar**	Small	78	22
			Medium	95	5
			Large	0	0
			District Average	**83**	**17**
		Tamil Nadu Average		**83**	**17**
ALL INDIA			Small	83	17
			Medium	83	17
			Large	83	17
			All India Average	**83**	**17**

Source: Primary Field Survey.

Perception on Livelihood Status Indicators

Table 6.13 shows the effect of increased returns from Bt cotton on farmers' livelihood status, through indicators like increased expenditure on education for their children, increased expenditure on the intake of high value nutritious food, increased expenditure on their recreation, increased expenditure on social functions and increased expenditure on the health of their family members and livestock. It was found that a high proportion of farmers reported that due to high returns from Bt cotton, they had used their increased income on such livelihood indicators. On average 85 per cent farmers invested in better quality education for their children, 72 per cent reported intake of high value and nutritious food, 81 per cent in recreation, 85 per cent in social functions, 75 per cent on health of their family members and 68 per cent on health of livestock. An exception is seen in case of Yavatmal district of Maharashtra which did not show a good performance as compared to other States and districts. As regards purchase of property, it was seen that a relatively lower proportion of farmers' (31%) reported that increased incomes did not result in their buying property. It is to be noted that in India, just farming in itself has not resulted in such high incomes so as to afford a high standard/luxurious of living to the extent of buying huge property, excepting in the case of large farmers. For this to happen non-farm activities need to develop in rural areas which has not happened in a big way so far.

Perception on Human and Livestock Health

When farmers were asked about health problems in their family members and livestock on account of Bt cotton, a huge proportion of them declined. However, a very small proportion of farmers in Gujarat, Maharashtra and Andhra Pradesh (less than 10%) reported this to be a problem (Table 6.14).

Table 6.13: Effect of Returns from Bt Cotton on Farmers' Livelihood Status

Regions	States	Districts	Farm Size Categories	Better Quality Education		Intake of High Value Foods		Recreational Activities		Social functions		Better Health Care Facilities of				Buying Property	
												Family		Livestock			
				Yes	No	Yes	No	Yes	No	Yes	No	Yes	No	Yes	No	Yes	No
	Punjab	Bathinda	Small	75	25	50	50	65	35	85	15	0	100	0	100	0	100
			Medium	78	22	60	40	73	27	96	4	4	96	4	96	2	98
			Large	60	40	40	60	100	0	100	0	0	100	0	100	0	100
			District Average	76	24	56	44	77	23	93	7	1	99	1	99	1	99
		Fazilka	Small	50	50	50	50	80	20	100	0	60	40	8	93	0	100
			Medium	100	0	100	0	100	0	100	0	88	12	60	40	8	92
			Large	100	0	100	0	100	0	100	0	100	0	80	20	20	80
			District Average	80	20	78	22	90	10	100	0	80	20	45	55	10	90
		Punjab Average		78	22	64	36	81	19	96	4	38	62	20	80	5	95
Northern Region	Haryana	Hissar	Small	88	13	88	13	88	13	63	38	88	13	88	13	13	88
			Medium	97	3	97	3	97	3	88	12	94	6	94	6	29	71
			Large	100	0	100	0	92	8	92	8	100	0	100	0	58	42
			District Average	94	6	94	6	93	7	80	20	93	7	93	7	29	71
		Sirsa	Small	100	0	97	3	97	3	100	0	97	3	95	5	24	76
			Medium	100	0	100	0	95	5	95	5	100	0	100	0	36	64
			Large	100	0	100	0	100	0	100	0	100	0	100	0	55	45
			District Average	100	0	99	1	97	3	98	2	99	1	98	2	40	60
		Haryana Average		97	3	96	4	95	5	89	11	96	4	96	4	36	64

(Contd.)

Table 6.13 (*Contd.*)

Regions	States	Districts	Farm Size Categories	Better Quality Education		Intake of High Value Foods		Recreational Activities		Social functions		Better Health Care Facilities of				Buying Property	
												Family		Livestock			
				Yes	No	Yes	No	Yes	No	Yes	No	Yes	No	Yes	No	Yes	No
	Rajasthan	Hanumangarh	Small	56	44	56	44	56	44	33	67	22	78	11	89	0	100
			Medium	88	12	56	44	100	0	72	28	0	100	0	100	0	100
			Large	100	0	67	33	100	0	100	0	67	33	33	67	0	100
			District Average	73	27	57	43	77	23	60	40	25	75	13	87	0	100
		Rajasthan Average		73	27	57	43	77	23	60	40	25	75	13	87	0	100
	Gujarat	Bhavnagar	Small	93	7	86	14	93	7	90	10	86	14	83	17	59	41
			Medium	92	8	89	11	89	11	92	8	89	11	65	35	46	54
			Large	100	0	100	0	100	0	100	0	100	0	75	25	75	25
			District Average	93	7	89	11	91	9	91	9	89	11	73	27	53	47
		Surendranagar	Small	88	13	88	13	90	10	88	13	69	31	33	67	25	75
			Medium	95	5	95	5	90	10	100	0	95	5	70	30	40	60
			Large	50	50	50	50	50	50	100	0	100	0	50	50	50	50
			District Average	80	20	79	21	77	23	91	9	87	13	56	44	35	65
		Gujarat Average		82	18	83	17	84	16	91	9	83	17	60	40	43	57
Central Region	Madhya Pradesh	Dhar	Small	95	5	95	5	95	5	95	5	95	5	95	5	5	95
			Medium	97	3	97	3	97	3	97	3	97	3	97	3	27	73
			Large	95	5	95	5	95	5	95	5	95	5	95	5	21	79
			District Average	96	4	96	4	96	4	96	4	96	4	96	4	19	81

(*Contd.*)

Table 6.13 (*Contd.*)

Regions	*States*	*Districts*	*Farm Size Categories*	*Better Quality Education*		*Intake of High Value Foods*		*Recreational Activities*		*Social functions*		*Better Health Care Facilities of*				*Buying Property*	
												Family		*Livestock*			
				Yes	*No*	*Yes*	*No*	*Yes*	*No*	*Yes*	*No*	*Yes*	*No*	*Yes*	*No*	*Yes*	*No*
		Khargone	Small	96	4	96	4	96	4	96	4	96	4	96	4	9	91
			Medium	100	0	100	0	100	0	100	0	100	0	100	0	9	91
			Large	93	7	93	7	93	7	93	7	93	7	93	7	7	93
			District Average	97	3	97	3	97	3	97	3	97	3	97	3	9	91
		Madhya Pradesh Average		96	4	96	4	96	4	96	4	96	4	96	4	14	86
	Maharashtra	Jalgaon	Small	33	67	33	67	24	76	33	67	40	60	38	62	11	89
			Medium	89	11	89	11	89	11	89	11	89	11	89	11	39	61
			Large	100	0	100	0	100	0	100	0	100	0	100	0	57	43
			District Average	70	30	72	28	71	29	74	26	75	25	72	28	30	70
		Yavatmal	Small	24	76	18	82	2	98	22	78	24	76	14	86	10	90
			Medium	73	27	73	27	73	27	73	27	73	27	73	27	52	48
			Large	80	20	80	20	80	20	80	20	80	20	80	20	80	20
			District Average	55	45	52	48	52	48	57	43	57	43	53	47	45	55
		Maharashtra Average		60	40	62	38	61	39	65	35	66	34	63	37	32	68
Southern Region	Andhra Pradesh	Adilabad	Small	100	0	100	0	100	0	100	0	100	0	100	0	100	0
			Medium	100	0	100	0	100	0	100	0	100	0	100	0	100	0
			Large	100	0	100	0	100	0	100	0	100	0	100	0	100	0
			District Average	100	0	100	0	100	0	100	0	100	0	100	0	100	0

(*Contd.*)

Table 6.13 (*Contd.*)

Regions	States	Districts	Farm Size Categories	Better Quality Education		Intake of High Value Foods		Recreational Activities		Social functions		Better Health Care Facilities of				Buying Property	
												Family		Livestock			
				Yes	No	Yes	No	Yes	No	Yes	No	Yes	No	Yes	No	Yes	No
		Warangal	Small	78	22	71	29	25	75	31	69	55	45	36	64	15	85
			Medium	92	8	77	23	46	54	54	46	69	31	54	46	15	85
			Large	100	0	100	0	50	50	100	0	100	0	100	0	50	50
			District Average	85	15	80	20	40	60	58	42	70	30	58	42	24	76
		Andhra Pradesh	Average	91	9	86	14	65	35	75	25	82	18	75	25	58	42
	Kamataka	Dharwad	Small	90	10	88	13	81	19	81	19	85	15	81	19	44	56
			Medium	95	5	95	5	89	11	95	5	95	5	95	5	53	47
			Large	100	0	100	0	67	33	67	33	100	0	67	33	33	67
			District Average	91	9	90	10	83	17	84	16	89	11	84	16	46	54
		Kamataka	Average	91	9	90	10	83	17	84	16	89	11	84	16	46	54
	Tamil Nadu	Virudunagar	Small	85	15	82	18	75	25	90	10	73	27	77	23	19	81
			Medium	89	11	90	10	80	20	95	5	75	25	83	17	25	75
			Large														
			District Average	87	13	85	15	77	23	92	8	74	26	81	19	20	80
		Tamil Nadu Average		87	13	85	15	77	23	92	8	74	26	81	19	20	80
All India			Small	77	23	73	27	71	29	74	26	66	34	57	43	22	78
			Medium	92	8	88	12	88	12	90	10	78	22	72	28	32	68
			Large	91	9	87	13	88	12	95	5	88	12	77	23	43	57
			All India Average	85	15	82	18	81	19	85	15	75	25	68	32	31	69

Source: Primary Field Survey.

Table 6.14: Health Problems and Diseases due to Bt Cotton in Humans (Family Members) and Livestock (%)

Regions	*States*	*Districts*	*Farm Size Categories*	*Family Members*		*Livestock*	
				Yes	*No*	*Yes*	*No*
Northern Region	**Punjab**	**Bathinda**	Small	0	100	0	100
			Medium	0	100	0	100
			Large	0	100	0	100
			District Average	**0**	**100**	**0**	**100**
		Fazilka	Small	0	100	0	100
			Medium	0	100	0	100
			Large	0	100	0	100
			District Average	**0**	**100**	**0**	**100**
		Punjab Average		**0**	**100**	**0**	**100**
	Haryana	**Hissar**	Small	0	100	0	100
			Medium	0	100	0	100
			Large	0	100	0	100
			District Average	**0**	**100**	**0**	**100**
		Sirsa	Small	0	100	0	100
			Medium	0	100	0	100
			Large	0	100	0	100
			District Average	**0**	**100**	**0**	**100**
		Haryana Average		**0**	**100**	**0**	**100**
	Rajasthan	**Hanumangarh**	Small	0	100	0	100
			Medium	0	100	0	100
			Large	0	100	0	100
			District Average	**0**	**100**	**0**	**100**
		Rajasthan Average		**0**	**100**	**0**	**100**
Central Region	**Gujarat**	**Bhavnagar**	Small	3	97	10	90
			Medium	3	97	5	95
			Large	0	100	0	100
			District Average	**2**	**98**	**6**	**94**
		Surendranagar	Small	4	96	2	98
			Medium	0	100	0	100
			Large	0	100	0	100
			District Average	**2**	**98**	**1**	**99**
		Gujarat Average		**2**	**98**	**4**	**96**
	Madhya Pradesh	**Dhar**	Small	0	100	0	100
			Medium	0	100	0	100
			Large	0	100	0	100
			District Average	**0**	**100**	**0**	**100**
		Khargone	Small	0	100	0	100
			Medium	0	100	0	100
			Large	0	100	0	100
			District Average	**0**	**100**	**0**	**100**
		Madhya Pradesh Average		**0**	**100**	**0**	**100**
	Maharashtra	**Jalgaon**	Small	0	100	7	93
			Medium	0	100	0	100
			Large	0	100	0	100
			District Average	**0**	**100**	**3**	**97**

(Contd.)

Table 6.14 (*Contd.*)

Regions	*States*	*Districts*	*Farm Size Categories*	*Family Members*		*Livestock*	
				Yes	*No*	*Yes*	*No*
		Yavatmal	Small	0	100	8	92
			Medium	0	100	0	100
			Large	0	100	40	60
			District Average	**0**	**100**	**14**	**86**
		Maharashtra Average		**0**	**100**	**6**	**94**
Southern Region	**Andhra Pradesh**	**Adilabad**	Small	0	100	8	92
			Medium	10	90	0	100
			Large	0	100	0	100
			District Average	**4**	**96**	**4**	**96**
		Warangal	Small	16	84	9	91
			Medium	8	92	15	85
			Large	0	100	0	100
			District Average	**10**	**90**	**10**	**90**
		Andhra Pradesh Average		**8**	**92**	**7**	**93**
	Karnataka	**Dharwad**	Small	0	100	0	100
			Medium	0	100	0	100
			Large	0	100	0	100
			District Average	**0**	**100**	**0**	**100**
		Karnataka Average		**0**	**100**	**0**	**100**
	Tamil Nadu	**Virudunagar**	Small	0	100	0	100
			Medium	0	100	0	100
			Large	—	—	—	—
			District Average	**0**	**100**	**0**	**100**
		Tamil Nadu Average		**0**	**100**	**0**	**100**
ALL INDIA			Small	2	98	3	97
			Medium	2	98	1	99
			Large	0	100	3	97
			All India Average	**2**	**98**	**2**	**98**

Source: Primary Field Survey.

Perception on Soil Quality

As regards soil quality (Table 6.15), 96 per cent farmers reported no effect of Bt cotton on soil quality across all surveyed regions and farm classes. However, less than 10 per cent farmers in each State also reported this to be a problem as they felt that soil salinity and alkalinity had increased.

Table 6.15: Bt Cotton and Soil Quality (%)

Regions	*States*	*Districts*	*Farm Size Categories*	*Effects Soil Quality*	*No Effect on Soil Quality*
Northern Region	**Punjab**	**Bathinda**	Small	0	100
			Medium	4	96
			Large	0	100
			District Average	**2**	**98**
		Fazilka	Small	10	90
			Medium	0	100
			Large	20	80
			District Average	**9**	**91**
		Punjab Average		**5**	**95**
	Haryana	**Hissar**	Small	0	100
			Medium	3	97
			Large	8	92
			District Average	**3**	**97**
		Sirsa	Small	3	97
			Medium	0	100
			Large	0	100
			District Average	**1**	**99**
		Haryana Average		**2**	**98**
	Rajasthan	**Hanumangarh**	Small	2	98
			Medium	8	92
			Large	10	90
			District Average	**7**	**93**
		Rajasthan Average		**7**	**93**
Central Region	**Gujarat**	**Bhavnagar**	Small	8	92
			Medium	3	97
			Large	5	95
			District Average	**5**	**95**
		Surendranagar	Small	3	97
			Medium	5	95
			Large	8	92
			District Average	**6**	**94**
		Gujarat Average		**4**	**96**
	Madhya Pradesh	**Dhar**	Small	5	95
			Medium	3	97
			Large	0	100
			District Average	**3**	**97**
		Khargone	Small	10	90
			Medium	9	91
			Large	0	100
			District Average	**6**	**94**
		Madhya Pradesh Average		**9**	**91**
	Maharashtra	**Jalgaon**	Small	9	91
			Medium	7	93
			Large	0	100
			District Average	**7**	**93**
		Yavatmal	Small	8	92
			Medium	13	87
			Large	0	100
			District Average	**9**	**91**
		Maharashtra Average		**8**	**92**

(Contd.)

(Contd.)

Regions	*States*	*Districts*	*Farm Size Categories*	*Effects Soil Quality*	*No Effect on Soil Quality*
Southern Region	**Andhra Pradesh**	**Adilabad**	Small	3	97
			Medium	2	98
			Large	0	100
			District Average	**2**	**98**
		Warangal	Small	5	95
			Medium	5	95
			Large	0	100
			District Average	**3**	**97**
		Andhra Pradesh Average		**2.5**	**97.5**
	Karnataka	**Dharwad**	Small	0	100
			Medium	0	100
			Large	0	100
			District Average	**0**	**100**
		Karnataka Average		**0**	**100**
	Tamil Nadu	**Virudunagar**	Small	0	100
			Medium	0	100
			Large	0	0
			District Average	**0**	**100**
		Tamil Nadu Average		**0**	**100**
ALL INDIA			Small	4	96
			Medium	4	96
			Large	5	95
			All India Average	**4**	**96**

Source: Primary Field Survey.

The overall economic impact of Bt cotton during the past 10 years has been positive and quite significant. Also, by and large, the farmers expressed a view that the overall social impact has been positive. However, in Gujarat, Maharashtra and Andhra Pradesh, some farmers (less than 10%) also reported that there were adverse effects of Bt cotton on human and animal health. Further, a small proportion of farmers (less than 10%) in all the surveyed States reported negative effects of Bt cotton on soil health on account of rising soil salinity and alkalinity. Hence, there is a need to do further research in those areas where farmers reported an adverse impact of Bt cotton on health and soil quality. However, it should be noted that the Bt cotton crops is highly susceptible to moisture stress and hence requires timely rainfall or good irrigation. Besides, the proliferation of hybrids is turning out to be a major menace in maintaining purity, arresting pest load and thereby complicating insect pest problems. The lack of knowledge of such scientific issues among farmers is resulting in soil toxicity and related health problems in certain years in some areas.

7

Impact of Bt Cotton on Labour Employment and Income of Landless Labourers

This chapter is based on the premise that if yields from Bt cotton has increased over the years, then the increased yields will result in an increase in labour days and labour wages, especially in the case of cotton picking. Therefore, this chapter attempts to see the impact of Bt cotton cultivation on the employment of labour and also on the income of landless labourers.

Human Labour Use in Cotton

Proportion of human labour cost to the total cost of Cotton was the highest in the cultivation of Cotton crop over the years. It ranged between 25 and 50 per cent. Also, Table 7.1 shows that after the advent of commercial Bt cotton cultivation in India, human labour use has increased compared to the Pre-Bt cotton period both in terms of growth rates and average mandays per hectare. On an average human labour use has increased from 96 Mandays/Hec in the Pre-Bt cotton period (1996-97 to 2001-02) to 104 Mandays/Hec in the Post-Bt cotton period (2002-03 to 2008-09) but showed a slight decline to 103 Mandays/Hec in the last 3 years of available data (2006-07 to 2008-09). Decline in labour use was observed only in the States of Andhra Pradesh and Tamil Nadu. The trend growth rates of human labour use has increased in Gujarat, Haryana, Karnataka and Maharashtra, while it has shown a decline in others especially Tamil Nadu. At the all India level also the rate of decline of human labour use has slowed down to –0.65 per cent from –1.59 per cent, which indicates some improvement over the Pre-Bt cotton period. It is found that over the years as 1 per cent increase in yields results in a 0.12 per cent increase in labour employment that is statistically significant at 5 per cent level of significance.

Table 7.1: Human Labour Use in Cotton Cultivation (Mandays/Hec)

States	1996-97	1997-98	1998-99	1999-2000	2000-01	2001-02	2002-03	2003-04	2004-05	2005-06	2006-07	2007-08	2008-09	Trend Growth Rates: Pre Bt Cotton Period (1996-97 to 2001-02)	Trend Growth Rates: Post Bt Cotton Period (2002-03 to 2008-09)	Averages: Pre Bt Cotton Period (1996-97 to 2001-02)	Averages: Post Bt Cotton Period (2002-03 to 2008-09)	Averages: 2006-2008 (Avg)
AP	125	127	105	83	111	105	110	117	125	113	103	82	105	–4.17	–3.64	109	108	97
Gujarat	99	105	108	92	67	105	100	140	134	147	121	124	158	–3.40	3.77	96	132	134
Haryana	74	61	72	101	91	59	81	90	96	90	96	100	99	3.22	3.43	80	96	98
Karnataka	84	76	91	85	92	94	84	72	84	82	87	89	85	3.16	1.71	87	83	87
MP	61	76	72	68	33	53	86	92	102	105	89	85	70	–9.00	–3.15	61	90	82
Maharashtra	108	105	103	105	98	107	106	104	98	100	105	109	104	–0.78	0.31	104	104	106
Punjab	103	72	76	91	88	85	91	99	101	89	104	100	90	1.98	–0.18	89	96	98
Rajasthan	72	70	68	66	58	75	76	77	74	74	87	85	70	1.29	–1.92	70	78	81
Tamil Nadu	202	187	171	169	164	195	186	192	158	122	149	121	149	–1.66	–5.67	181	154	140
All India Avg	**103**	**98**	**96**	**96**	**89**	**98**	**102**	**109**	**108**	**102**	**105**	**100**	**103**	**–1.59**	**–0.65**	**96**	**104**	**103**

Source: Directorate of Economics and Statistics, Ministry of Agriculture and Cooperation.

Hence, from Table 7.1 it is seen that human labour use has shown some improvement since the Bt cotton period. It was also seen from the field data that labour availability is becoming a major problem in the Cotton cultivating regions. This is mainly due to absorption of labour under the Mahatma Gandhi National Rural Employment Guarantee Act. With MNREGA providing 100 days of guaranteed work, timely availability of labourers especially during the Cotton picking season is seen as a problem. Farmers feel that the labour shortage has been pushing labour costs upwards.

On the basis of available data from the Ministry of Agriculture (Table 7.2) on family and hired labour days, it is seen that the all India average hired labour days are slightly more (54.14 Labour days/Hec) than family labour days (49.88 Labour days/Hec). Further, the trend growth rates of hired labour (0.89%) are lesser than family labour (–2.39%).

Table 7.2: Family and Hired Labour Days/Hec in Cotton Cultivation

Family Labour Days/Hec	*2004-05*	*2005-06*	*2006-07*	*2007-08*	*2008-09*	*Trend Growth Rates (%)*
Andhra Pradesh	46.07	55.76	27.17	18.09	34.27	–15.78
Gujarat	71.11	64.93	54.50	51.56	74.39	–1.39
Haryana	70.00	61.99	61.19	64.94	60.18	–2.52
Karnataka	29.67	22.39	29.65	26.92	25.92	–0.86
Madhya Pradesh	79.34	73.31	46.14	50.62	35.28	–18.06
Maharashtra	27.64	34.26	37.24	39.12	36.20	6.96
Punjab	49.69	33.68	39.28	37.55	28.19	–9.74
Rajasthan	54.06	63.48	70.28	66.69	55.42	1.00
Tamil Nadu	60.62	41.00	75.24	57.64	102.07	14.83
All India Avg	54.24	50.09	48.96	45.89	50.22	**–2.39**
Hired Labour Days/Hec	*2004-05*	*2005-06*	*2006-07*	*2007-08*	*2008-09*	*Trend Growth Rates (%)*
Andhra Pradesh	78.74	57.61	75.89	63.93	70.98	–1.03
Gujarat	63.06	81.82	66.41	72.37	84.03	4.62
Haryana	25.68	27.67	35.01	35.30	38.78	11.27
Karnataka	54.66	59.26	57.45	62.48	58.58	1.93
Madhya Pradesh	22.62	31.49	43.29	34.40	35.15	10.19
Maharashtra	70.26	66.16	67.72	69.52	68.00	–0.16
Punjab	51.22	55.52	64.74	62.87	61.53	5.04
Rajasthan	19.91	10.65	16.88	18.61	34.30	17.90
Tamil Nadu	96.89	80.96	73.55	63.27	47.35	–15.45
All India Avg	53.67	52.34	55.65	53.65	55.40	**0.89**

Source: Directorate of Economics and Statistics, Ministry of Agriculture and Cooperation.

Impact on Wages of Landless Labourers

As regards the impact of Bt cotton on wages of landless labourers is concerned (Table 7.3), it is seen that the average daily wages of landless labourers increased by more than 80 per cent from the Pre-Bt cotton to the Post-Bt cotton period, for all kinds of farm operations, in the surveyed regions. Male labour wages in absolute terms were higher than female labour wages in both the Pre as well as the Post- Bt cotton period, and the wage gap increased slightly in the Post-Bt cotton period. The percentage change in female labour wages increased significantly in the Post-Bt cotton period such that the percentage increase in female labour wages was found to be 10 times more (all operations) than their male counterparts. It is also seen that at the all India level labour wages have been highest for post-harvesting operations followed by picking. Moreover, the daily wage rates of labourers in the Cotton cultivating regions are much higher than the national averages provided by the Ministry of Labour and Environment, Government of India. The revised wage rate of MNREGA w.e.f. 1-06-2009 was an average of ₹ 100/day, while the average daily wage rates in agricultural operations in rural areas in 2009 was around ₹ 83/day wage rate. From the field survey the average wages of male and female labour together in cotton cultivation was found to be around ₹ 180/day.

Perception of Wage Labourers on Livelihood Status Indicators

It would be seen from Table 7.4 that, at the all India level a high proportion of landless labourers reported greater expenditure on livelihood activities due to relatively higher returns from Bt cotton. On average 89 per cent farmers invested in better quality education for their children, 79 per cent reported intake of high value and nutritious food, 67 per cent in recreation, 66 per cent in social functions, 85 per cent on health of their family members and 72 per cent on health of livestock. Higher expenditure on education and high value food was reported by majority farmers in all the surveyed regions. However, higher expenditures on social function, recreational activities and better health care facilities were reported by majority farmers in most regions excepting some.

Table 7.3: Average Daily Wages of Landless Labourers (₹/Day)

Regions	States	Districts	Farm Operations	Female Labourers		Male Labourers		Percentage Increase	
				Pre-Bt Cotton	Post Bt-Cotton	Pre-Bt Cotton	Post Bt-Cotton	Female Labourers	Male Labourers
Northern Region	Punjab	Bathinda	Ploughing & Sowing	88	165	55	160	87.50	190.91
			Fertilising	150	250	113	218	66.67	93.10
			Irrigation	93	180	113	185	93.55	63.72
			Weeding	87	168	55	160	93.10	190.91
			Pesticide Spraying	86	161	86	220	87.21	155.81
			Picking	50	141	48	143	181.00	197.92
			Post-Harvesting	83	174	55	160	109.64	190.91
		Fazilka	Ploughing & Sowing	150	250	113	218	66.67	93.10
			Fertilising	91	155	99	171	70.33	72.73
			Irrigation	94	181	114	186	92.55	63.16
			Weeding	100	231	104	225	130.56	117.24
			Pesticide Spraying	85	160	120	270	88.24	125.00
			Picking	56	239	79	279	330.63	254.55
			Post-Harvesting	83	175	130	290	110.84	123.08
	Haryana	Hissar	Ploughing & Sowing	80	170	150	250	112.50	66.67
			Fertilising	91	154	111	180	62.93	62.16
			Irrigation	93	182	100	169	97.50	69.00
			Weeding	87	167	115	165	91.95	43.48
			Pesticide Spraying	100	186	110	196	86.00	78.18
			Picking	81	172	71	157	112.33	121.13
			Post-Harvesting	37	75	102	251	102.70	146.08
		Sirsa	Ploughing & Sowing	128	283	209	261	120.78	25.00
			Fertilising	111	280	200	267	153.39	33.33
			Irrigation	119	340	250	325	185.71	30.00
			Weeding	137	336	229	299	144.79	30.94
			Pesticide Spraying	108	295	228	358	173.15	57.36
			Picking	145	234	144	211	61.21	46.15
			Post-Harvesting	119	269	209	285	126.32	36.12

(*Contd.*)

Table 7.3 (*Contd.*)

Regions	States	Districts	Farm Operations	Female Labourers		Male Labourers		Percentage Increase	
				Pre-Bt Cotton	Post Bt-Cotton	Pre-Bt Cotton	Post Bt-Cotton	Female Labourers	Male Labourers
	Rajasthan	Hanumangarh	Ploughing & Sowing	60	163	88	183	172.22	108.57
			Fertilising	90	155	100	170	72.22	70.00
			Irrigation	92	180	114	185	95.65	62.28
			Weeding	72	165	150	300	129.17	100.00
			Pesticide Spraying	70	150	190	316	114.29	66.12
			Picking	114	253	135	269	120.87	99.07
			Post-Harvesting	113	267	140	283	135.29	102.38
Certral Region	Gujarat	Bhavnagar	Ploughing & Sowing	94	165	107	160	75.53	49.53
			Fertilising	110	170	111	183	54.55	64.86
			Irrigation	104	195	105	168	87.50	60.00
			Weeding	96	166	100	150	73.82	50.00
			Pesticide Spraying	122	215	133	219	76.23	65.28
			Picking	106	163	108	154	53.77	42.59
			Post-Harvesting	83	175	100	213	110.84	112.50
		Surendranagar	Ploughing & Sowing	129	187	131	178	45.56	35.88
			Fertilising	156	210	138	194	35.00	40.58
			Irrigation	151	229	157	229	51.66	45.86
			Weeding	154	216	139	206	40.26	48.20
			Pesticide Spraying	154	230	159	256	48.92	61.01
			Picking	155	229	145	216	48.24	48.97
			Post-Harvesting	180	250	117	217	38.89	85.71
	Madhya Pradesh	Dhar	Ploughing & Sowing	100	210	100	210	110.00	110.00
			Fertilising	53	84	50	84	58.49	68.00
			Irrigation	93	150	82	150	61.29	82.93
			Weeding	117	205	105	200	75.21	90.48
			Pesticide Spraying	68	105	55	91	54.41	65.45
			Picking	118	220	108	220	86.44	103.70
			Post-Harvesting	84	174	108	215	107.14	99.07

(*Contd.*)

Table 7.3 *(Contd.)*

Regions	States	Districts	Farm Operations	Female Labourers		Male Labourers		Percentage Increase	
				Pre-Bt Cotton	Post Bt-Cotton	Pre-Bt Cotton	Post Bt-Cotton	Female Labourers	Male Labourers
		Khargone	**Ploughing & Sowing**	100	150	100	153	50.00	53.00
			Fertilising	70	100	70	100	42.86	42.86
			Irrigation	150	180	150	180	20.00	20.00
			Weeding	80	120	80	120	50.00	50.00
			Pesticide Spraying	53	84	50	85	58.49	70.00
			Picking	150	200	150	205	33.33	36.67
			Post-Harvesting	84	175	108	214	108.33	98.15
	Maharashtra	**Jalgaon**	**Ploughing & Sowing**	100	150	94	150	50.00	59.09
			Fertilising	84	124	77	144	47.62	88.41
			Irrigation	83	150	91	151	80.00	65.85
			Weeding	68	117	74	126	72.06	68.66
			Pesticide Spraying	99	150	94	150	52.17	58.82
			Picking	150	257	113	238	71.33	111.11
			Post-Harvesting	83	174	109	216	109.64	98.17
		Yavatmal	**Ploughing & Sowing**	52	96	82	185	84.62	125.61
			Fertilising	48	100	79	170	108.33	115.19
			Irrigation	55	105	93	195	90.91	109.68
			Weeding	58	117	81	162	101.72	100.00
			Pesticide Spraying	57	117	119	245	105.26	105.88
			Picking	88	193	88	175	118.75	98.86
			Post-Harvesting	71	135	108	220	90.14	103.70
Southern Region	**Andhra Pradesh**	**Adilabad**	**Ploughing & Sowing**	70	120	78	192	71.43	146.15
			Fertilising	72	124	84	190	72.22	126.19
			Irrigation	100	200	80	183	100.00	129.17
			Weeding	80	128	86	190	60.00	120.93
			Pesticide Spraying	86	131	88	177	52.33	101.14
			Picking	90	128	94	177	42.22	88.30
			Post-Harvesting	100	200	96	194	100.00	103.49

(Contd.)

Table 7.3 (*Contd.*)

Regions	States	Districts	Farm Operations	Female Labourers		Male Labourers		Percentage Increase	
				Pre-Bt Cotton	Post Bt-Cotton	Pre-Bt Cotton	Post Bt-Cotton	Female Labourers	Male Labourers
		Warangal	Ploughing & Sowing	53	108	119	294	104.76	147.66
			Fertilising	49	106	61	156	117.65	155.10
			Irrigation	36	100	71	159	175.86	123.94
			Weeding	49	118	74	130	140.82	75.68
			Pesticide Spraying	34	100	95	210	194.12	121.05
			Picking	51	116	100	176	127.45	76.00
			Post-Harvesting	30	100	65	137	233.33	110.26
	Karnataka	Dharwad	Ploughing & Sowing	41	67	59	99	64.91	69.23
			Fertilising	39	70	64	104	80.65	62.50
			Irrigation	42	158	60	95	280.00	58.33
			Weeding	41	91	77	120	124.66	55.56
			Pesticide Spraying	41	100	66	104	142.42	57.58
			Picking	47	114	70	163	140.38	133.33
			Post-Harvesting	25	100	71	120	300.00	68.00
	Tamil Nadu	Virudunagar	Ploughing & Sowing	88	188	122	222	113.64	82.19
			Fertilising	150	250	133	233	66.67	75.27
			Irrigation	92	180	125	225	95.65	80.00
			Weeding	80	176	83	183	120.31	121.21
			Pesticide Spraying	125	225	106	206	80.00	94.34
			Picking	80	180	90	190	125.00	111.11
			Post-Harvesting	75	175	108	215	133.33	99.07
India			**Ploughing & Sowing**	**89**	**165**	**107**	**194**	**85.47**	**81.53**
			Fertilising	**91**	**156**	**99**	**171**	**71.29**	**72.25**
			Irrigation	**93**	**181**	**114**	**186**	**93.66**	**63.44**
			Weeding	**87**	**168**	**103**	**182**	**93.21**	**76.33**
			Pesticide Spraying	**86**	**161**	**113**	**207**	**86.88**	**82.67**
			Picking	**99**	**189**	**103**	**198**	**91.61**	**92.69**
			Post-Harvesting	**83**	**174**	**108**	**215**	**109.37**	**98.62**

Source: Primary Field Survey.

Table 7.4: Impact of Bt Cotton Returns on Livelihood Status of Landless Labourers (%)

Region	States	Districts	Better Quality Education		Intake of High Value Foods		Recreational Activities		Social Functions		Better Health Care Facilities of			
											Family		Livestock	
			Expenditure Increased	Expenditure Decreased	Expenditure Increased	Expenditure Decreased	Expenditure Increased	Expenditure Decreased	Expenditure Increased	Expenditure Decreased	Expenditure Increased	Expenditure Decreased	Expenditure Increased	Expenditure Decreased
Northern Region	Punjab	Bathinda	95	5	90	10	45	55	80	20	55	45	100	0
		Fazilka	90	10	95	5	80	20	85	15	60	40	65	35
	Haryana	Hissar	95	5	75	25	80	20	40	60	95	5	55	45
		Sirsa	95	5	85	15	80	20	70	30	85	15	75	25
	Rajasthan	Hanumangarh	90	10	50	50	75	25	70	30	100	0	100	0
Central Region	Gujarat	Bhavnagar	90	10	90	10	85	15	95	5	95	5	65	35
		Surendranagar	90	10	75	25	80	20	75	25	90	10	90	10
	Madhya Pradesh	Dhar	90	10	90	10	65	35	65	35	90	10	65	35
		Khargone	85	15	80	20	80	20	80	20	80	20	80	20
	Maharashtra	Jalgaon	90	10	100	0	90	10	85	15	100	0	100	0
		Yavatmal	95	5	95	5	5	95	0	100	95	5	100	0
Southern Region	Andhra Pradesh	Adilabad	90	10	100	0	95	5	90	10	100	0	90	10
		Warangal	85	15	65	35	20	80	20	80	70	30	25	75
	Karnataka	Dharwad	90	10	80	20	80	20	90	10	95	5	60	40
	Tamil Nadu	Virudunagar	92	8	82	18	80	20	90	10	90	10	90	10
All India Average			89	11	79	21	67	33	66	34	85	15	72	28

Source: Primary Field Survey.

8

Key Findings and Conclusions

It becomes clear from the foregoing discussion that the Bt cotton experience presents a mixed picture—a success from the point of view of improvement in farm yields and incomes in most places, but its ecological sustainability and economic advantage for small farmers in the long run are questionable. The yield of cotton has substantially increased in the past one decade due to the adoption of Bt cotton as well as irrigation and favourable output prices. The input prices and cost of production of cotton also increased in the recent years. But still there is good margin in most places, although farmers in some regions, especially Maharashtra and Madhya Pradesh, continue to face low and unstable cotton prices, high input costs and low or no margin in some cases.

The average per hectare cost of cultivation in the country increased by about 68 per cent in the post- Bt cotton period, while the average net returns rose by nearly 375 per cent. The high costs in Bt cotton were mainly due to rise in the cost of human labour, followed by fertilizers, seeds, pesticides and mechanization. Using the data of the Ministry of Agriculture, Government of India, the average net return per hectare between 2006-07 to 2008-09 was the highest in Gujarat (₹ 12,767 per hectare) and lowest in Maharashtra (₹ 1,143 per hectare). It was also observed during the field survey that most of the Bt cotton growers across the country were small and marginal farmers.

One of the reasons why farmers adopted Bt cotton was that it would help in protecting the crop against the most damaging bollworms by significantly reducing chemical insecticide use and also reducing the risk of crop failures. It was found that pesticide consumption in the country dropped by almost 23 per cent in the post-Bt cotton period. The proportion of insecticide cost to the total cost of cultivation in the cotton growing States showed an overall declining trend, although there is a slight increase in it in the recent years, due mainly to the emergence of several sucking pests such as Jassids, White flies, Thrips and Mealy bugs as well as bacterial, fungal and viral diseases, which could not be controlled by the current Bt varieties. In some cases even bollworms showed signs of resistance to Bt technology. This is indeed a cause for concern.

No doubt, the yields of cotton in India have almost doubled in the post-Bt period, but still there is a big difference in India's best Bt yields as compared to yields of cotton crop in some other countries such as Australia, Israel, Mexico, China and Brazil.

It was further observed that the average area under cotton was highest in the State of Maharashtra, but there was no commensurate increase in the yield of cotton in the recent years. The average yield of cotton in Maharashtra continued to be as low as 319 kg-lint per hectare as against 714 kg-lint per hectare in Tamil Nadu and 648 kg-lint per hectare in Gujarat. In fact large pockets of cotton area in Maharashtra and Madhya Pradesh are rainfed with shallow soils and erratic rainfall patterns which affect the crop yield. Therefore, there is a need for close examination of the suitability of these areas for Bt cotton as farmers at present are not properly guided in this respect. As a matter of fact, water stress affects transgenes in crops and has serious implications such as:

(i) ineffective pest controls,
(ii) pest becoming resistant to the Bt toxin, and
(iii) high pesticide use.

The lack of knowledge of such scientific issues among farmers result in soil toxicity related health problems. The issue whether Bt cotton can contribute to ecological safety by decreasing pesticide use under varying agro-climatic situations is questionable.

Currently only about 30 per cent of the cotton area in the country is irrigated. Bt cotton is more suitable under assured irrigation and, therefore, the economics of Bt cotton should be seen against the rising irrigation cost on account of increased diesel cost as well as social, ecological and opportunity cost. Besides, Bt is found to be associated with higher use of chemical fertilizers causing a threat to soil health.

Bt cotton is a labour intensive crop and hence farmers find it difficult to cultivate cotton in places where there is labour scarcity and high wage rates of labour. Mechanisation can provide an answer but currently there are no small farmer friendly mechanical innovations.

While the seed rate of cotton seems to have declined in the recent years, due to Bt varieties, the proportion of seed cost to total cost have shown increasing trends in most States in recent years. The all India average seed cost increased from ₹ 650 per kg in the year 2005-06 to ₹ 1239 per kg in 2008-09. Also farmers have to purchase Bt seeds every year at a higher rate which causes hardship and disincentive to the small farmers. Besides, at present above 800 varieties of Bt seeds are marketed by different private companies by paying royalty to Monsanto, a multi-national seed company that had developed the first generation GM crop and hence has a patent for the Bt gene. Such proliferation of hybrid seeds results in complicated insect and pest problems, affecting cotton yields. At the same time any monopolistic behaviour of seed market is bound to be anti-farmers. Therefore, some kind of regulation of seed varieties and their prices may be necessary. Also unavailability of high yielding quality of Bt cotton seeds seemed to affect yields of cotton in several places, especially Surendranagar in Gujarat and Hanumangarh in Rajasthan.

As regards perception of farmers on various issues of Bt cotton, about 95 per cent farmers said that Bt cotton yields were higher than Non-Bt cotton and 88 per cent said that returns were also higher. 85 per cent farmers said that the quantity of seed usage per hectare on Bt cotton was less than that used in Non-Bt cotton. However, 93 per cent farmers said that the expenditure on Bt cotton seeds was more than Non-Bt cotton. About 4 per cent farmers said that they had faced problems of spurious seeds. Most of the states conformed to this, except Gujarat, wherein 21 per cent farmers said that they had faced such a problem. This was very similar across all the surveyed districts and across different farm size categories. It was observed that nearly 85 per cent farmers did not plant 'refuge crops' alongside their Bt cotton plots. This was partly because of lack of farmers' knowledge regarding the importance of refuge crops in protecting the Bt cotton, and partly on account of small farmers' inability and unwillingness to leave any area for refuge, aiming at getting higher yields and income on maximum areas. Further, the proportions were generally skewed towards large farmers in most of the surveyed districts. This meant that small farmers were taking more risk by devoting the entire area to Bt cotton in order to derive immediate maximum benefits. A relatively higher proportion of farmers (54%), reported greater fertilizer usage on Bt cotton compared to Non Bt-cotton. At the all India level, 77 per cent farmers reported that the quantity of pesticide usage on Bt cotton had reduced over the years, and 79 per cent said that the expenditure on pesticide use for Bt cotton had also reduced. However, a relatively higher proportion of farmers (63%) in the Hanumangarh district of Rajasthan, Yavatmal district of Maharashtra (90%) and Virudunagar district of Tamil Nadu (79%) reported an increase in pesticide usage and a commensurate increase in pesticide expenditure. As regards the role of Bt cotton in minimizing the attack of Bollworms, 90 per cent farmers claimed that Bt cotton had reduced the attack of Bollworms. Only in certain regions like Sirsa, Dharwad and Virudunagar, relatively higher proportion of farmers (30-40%) reported that the attacks of

Bollworm had increased. As regards irrigation expenditure, a relatively higher proportion of farmers (65%) said that irrigation expenditure on Bt cotton was higher than Non-Bt cotton.

On the issue of farmers' suicides, 5 per cent small farmers in Jalgaon and Yavatmal districts of Maharashtra and 3 per cent medium farmers in Adilabad district and 2 per cent small farmers in the Warangal district of Andhra Pradesh reported farm related suicide within their families. Farmers in the central Indian region blamed the suicides mainly on low and erratic nature of rainfall as this was a rainfed region without much irrigation facilities, unavailability of timely credit and low and fluctuating Cotton prices over the years that made production risky in certain years.

The field survey documented the effect of increased returns from Bt cotton on the livelihood status of farmers and landless labourers through various indicators. It was found that a high proportion of farmers reported that relatively high returns from Bt cotton had resulted in higher spending on nutritious food, health of their family members, health of livestock, etc. At the same time the incomes were not high enough to afford a high standard of living excepting in the case of large farmers.

The overall economic impact of Bt cotton during the past 10 years was perceived to be positive and quite significant. Also, by and large, the farmers expressed a view that the overall social impact has been positive. However, in Gujarat, Maharashtra and Andhra Pradesh, some farmers (less than 10%) also reported that there were adverse effects of Bt Cotton on human and animal health, although they could not explicitly mention that why and how of it. Further, a small proportion of farmers (less than 10%) in all the surveyed States reported negative effects of Bt cotton on soil quality on account of rising soil salinity and alkalinity. Hence, there is a need to do further research in those areas where farmers reported an adverse impact of Bt cotton on health and soil quality.

Conclusions and Policy Implications

Based on the analysis of both secondary and primary data, it may be concluded by saying that the adoption of Bt cotton has helped improve the farm productivity and incomes in most of the irrigated areas, while stagnation in yields of cotton continue in several rainfed areas. In fact, Bt cotton should not be looked at as a magic bullet, as bollworm can develop resistance to it and also other pests can take over. Also increased use of chemical fertilizers in Bt cotton fields is a cause for concern from the point of view of ecological sustainability. Therefore, promoting balanced use of nutrients, organic as well as inorganic would be important. At the same time GM technologies can help meet the challenge of climate change in maintaining biotic as well as abiotic stresses, which can be explored and utilized.

Bio-safety aspect of Bt crops is another area of concern. At present, there is neither an appropriate policy framework nor architecture for regulation. In fact, there is a need to reform and improve bio-safety testing and monitoring system in the country.

Moreover, India is gifted with bio-diversity while gene technology may restrict bio-diversity. Also, growing deskilling of farmers, reduced choices and compromised seed quality remain areas of concern which the country's policy makers need to address.

Bibliography

All India Coordinated Cotton Improvement Project (2010), Central Institute for Cotton Research (CICR), Nagpur

Bhargava, Pushpa M. (2003), 'High Stakes in Agro Research—Resisting the Push', *Economic & Political Weekly*, August 23.

Bhargava, Pushpa M. (2009), 'Insufficient Regulatory Supervision Prior to Release of Genetically Modified Crops for Commercial Cultivation in India', *Journal of Bioscience*, Indian Academy of Sciences (http://www.ias.ac.in/jbiosci/june2009/pp167–168/annex.pdf).

Blaise, D. and K.R. Kranthi (2011), 'Cry1Ac Expression in Transgenic Bt Cotton Hybrids is Influenced by Soil Moisture and Depth', *Current Science*, Vol. 101, No. 6, September 25.

Coalition for a GM Free India (2011), 'India's "Public Sector Indigenous GM Cotton—A Scientific Fraud' (http://www.indiaenvironmentportal.org.in/files/file/Coalition%20for%20a%20GM%20Free%20India.doc)

Choudhary, B. and Gaur, K. (2010), 'Bt Cotton in India: A Country Profile', International Service for the Acquisition of Agri-biotech Applications (ISAAA). Series of Biotech Crop Profiles, Ithaca, NY.

FICCI, 'Cotton 2020 – Roadmap for Sustainable Production', February 2012.

Gaurav, S., and Srijit Mishra (2012), 'To Bt or Not to Bt? Risk and Uncertainty Considerations in Technology Assessment,' Indira Gandhi Institute of Development Research, Mumbai, January 2012, http://www.igidr.ac.in/pdf/publication/WP-2012-001.pdf.

Goswami, B., (2007), 'Making a Meal of Bt cotton' (http://infochangeindia.org,other/features/making-a-meal-of-bt-cotton.html).

Herring, Ronald J. (2005), 'Miracle Seeds, Suicide Seeds, and the Poor: GMOs, NGOs, Farmers, and the State', in Social Movements in India: Poverty, Power and Politics, ed. Raka Ray and Mary Katzenstein. Lanham, Md.: Rowman and Littlefield/New Delhi: Oxford University Press.

Herring, Ronald J., and N. Chandrasekhara Rao (2012), 'On the 'Failure of Bt Cotton—Analysing a Decade of Experience', *Economic & Political Weekly*, May 5, Vol. XLVII, No.18.

International Service for the Acquisition of Agri-biotech Applications (ISAAA) Briefs, Brief 41 (2009) and Brief 42 (2010), Ithaca NY.

Kranthi, Keshav R., S. Naidu, C.S. Dhawad, A. Tatwawadi, K. Mate, E. Patil, A. A. Bharose, G.T. Behere, R.M. Wadaskar, and S. Kranthi (2005), 'Temporal and Intra-Plant Variability of Cry1Ac Expression in Bt-cotton and its Influence on the Survival of the Cotton Bollworm, *Helicoverpa ameriga* (Hübner) (Noctuidae: Lepidoptera)', *Current Science*, 89: 291–98.

Kuruganti, K. (2009), 'Bt Cotton and the Myth of Enhanced Yields', *Economic & Political Weekly*, May 30, Vol. XLIV, No. 22.

Manjunath, T.M., (2007), 'Bt-Cotton in India: Remarkable Adoption and Benefits', *Foundation for Biotechnology Awareness and Education*, Maryland, USA.

Mayer, C.D and Bhagirath Choudhary (2013), Adoption and Uptake Pathways of Bt Cotton in India, *Indian Society for Cotton Improvement*, Mumbai.

Ministry of Labour and Environment, Government of India.

Ministry of Agriculture and Cooperation, Department of Economics and Statistics, Government of India.

Mitra, S. and Sangeeta Shroff (2007), 'Farmers' Suicides in Maharashtra', *Economic & Political Weekly*, December 8.

Naik, Gopal, Matin Qaim, Arjunan Subramanian and David Zilberman (2005)' 'Bt Cotton Controversy—Some Paradoxes Explained', *Economic and Political Weekly*, April 9, (1514-1517).

Pray, C.E., Bengali, P., and Ramaswami, B. (2005). 'The Cost of Biosafety Regulations: The Indian Experience'. *Quarterly Journal of International Agriculture*, 44, 267-289.

Ramasundaram, P. and Hemchandra Gajbhiye (2001), 'Constraints to Cotton Production In India', Central Institute of Cotton Research (CICR) Technical Bulletin No. 19.

Ramasundaram, P., A. Suresh and Ramesh Chand (2011), 'Manipulating Technology for Surplus Extraction: The Case of Bt Cotton in India', *Economic & Political Weekly*, October 22, Vol. XLVI, No. 43.

Stone, Glenn Davis (2012), 'Ugly Facts about Bt Cotton Yields, Field Questions', February 12 http://www.gmwatch.eu/component/content/article/13699.

The Hindu Business Line (2010), 'Monsanto Begins Work on Bollgard III, Roundup Ready Flex', 09 March (http://www.thehindubusinessline.com/todays-paper/tp-agri-biz-and-commodity/article986045.ece)

UNCTAD Statistics, United Nations Conference on Trade and Development.

USDA, United States Department of Agriculture.

Index